SILICON VALLEY: *THE HISTORY IN PICTURES*

BY

MARY WADDEN

Post C

THIS SPACE MAY BE USED FOR CORRESPONDENCE

As someone born and raised in Los Altos who has spent her adult life as a commercial real estate broker in Silicon Valley, it struck me. Sure, this is the birthplace of the semiconductor and the Internet, but why did these inventions, which have transformed modern society, originate here and not anywhere else? While researching the answer to this question, I uncovered a rich and complex history that I thought could be told with images and memorabilia, bringing the story alive. Looking back, I wonder if part of the reason I felt empowered to take on such a project was due in part to the entrepreneurial spirit that helped shape this Valley. Perhaps. Once I embarked on this project, I became acutely aware of why I could write this book now but couldn't have conceived of it 20 years ago. My three pound Macbook Air possesses the processing power of all of the government computers running in the 1960s, combined. The access I have to the Adobe Suite of design applications provided me with publishing tools once only reserved for multinational corporations. Lastly, a large majority of the research I was able to do online. When I found myself confronted with questions like, 'What is the difference between a transistor and a microprocessor?' Google helped me navigate to the answer. I am blessed to live in such a wonderful and dynamic place. This is my tribute.

Please feel free to reach out to me directly with any questions or comments: marycwadden@gmail.com.

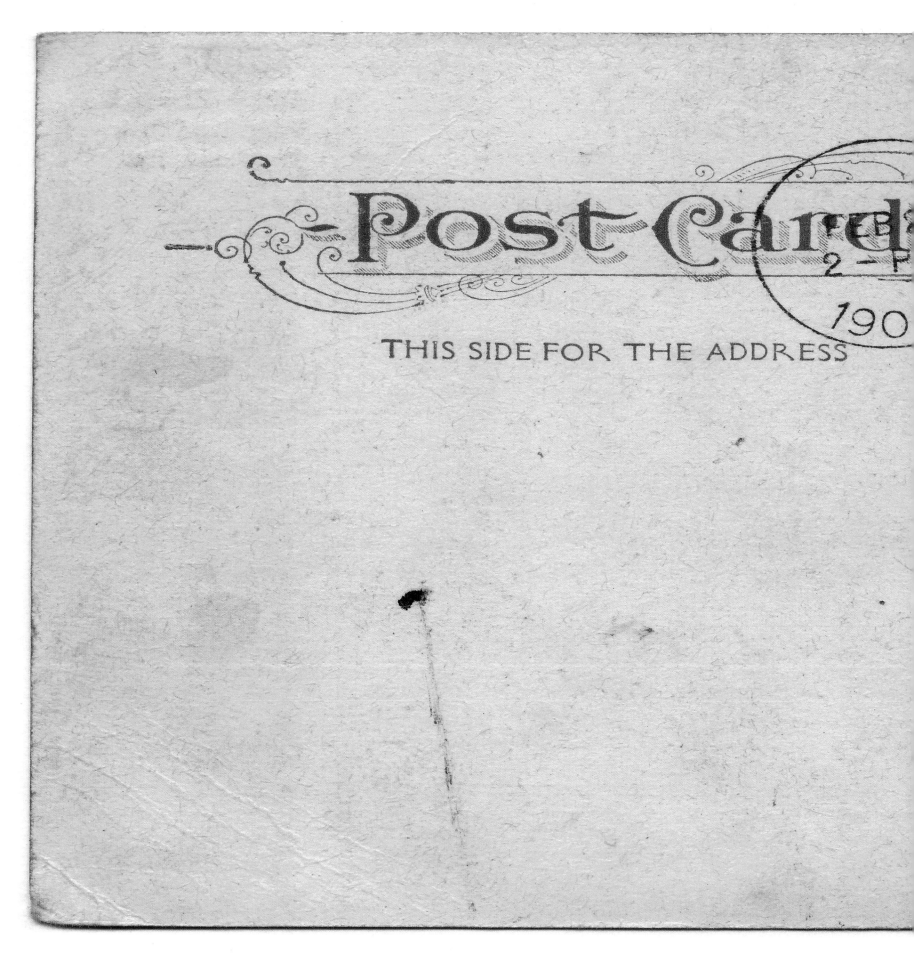

Post Card

2 - P

190

THIS SIDE FOR THE ADDRESS

ACKNOWLEDGMENTS

So many people have supported me throughout this endeavor. I would specifically like to thank:

My mother and sister, Rosemary and Elizabeth Wadden, for providing design and visual help.

My faithful editors, Rosemary Wadden, Dick Genest and John McLaughlin for taking this book from good to great.

All of my friends, family and colleagues who believed in the project from the very beginning, especially Dick Genest.

Lastly, this book would not have been possible at all if it wasn't for the numerous organizations and corporations who provided images, insight and wisdom to complete this book, including but not limited to:

John McLaughlin with the Silicon Valley Historical Association

The Historical Societies of Menlo Park, Palo Alto, Los Altos, Mountain View, Sunnyvale, Santa Clara & Saratoga

The Stanford Special Collections and University Archives

SJSU Special Collections & The California Room, San Jose Public Library

David Choice with ChoiceWay Media & NAIOP Silicon Valley

CONTENTS

Downtown Saratoga, late 1800s. *Saratoga Historical Society.*

WARNING!

NOTICE IS GIVEN that any person found Pilfering, Stealing, Robbing, or committing any act of Lawless Violence will be summarily

HANGED

Vigilance Committee.

MUNSON & WRIGHT, PRINT.

The modern age of California began in the mid 1700s with the arrival of Spanish missionaries. The following 100 years were a transformative time for Santa Clara Valley as the land essentially changed hands three separate times during that period: first from the native Ohlone population to the Spanish Missionaries, then from the Missionaries to Mexican Rancheros and finally from the Rancheros to the 49'ers who arrived in search of gold. This era was marked by a tremendous influx of settlers and was truly the Wild West.

ONE: THE WILD WEST

MISSION SANTA CLARA

Mission Santa Clara today, in the middle of Santa Clara University.

In the sixteenth century, Spain conquered the Aztec civilization in present day Mexico and spent the next 300 years in a quest for empire in the New World. In 1769 a group of Spanish Missionaries led by Junipero Serra set out to continue the line of missions into Alta California. Between 1769 and 1823, 21 missions were established as a way to gain empire for the crown of Spain. The route between the missions was named El Camino Real, "The Royal Way," as a tribute to the Spanish royalty who financed the quest. The Mission of Santa Clara was established in 1777 as the eighth mission and was originally constructed near the Guadalupe River. In the early years, it was destroyed and rebuilt five times prior to the final mission that exists today. Prior to the arrival of the missionaries, the Ohlone people lived near the bay for thousands of years. Unlike the Aztecs and Mayans, the Ohlone didn't build large cities but lived in small settlements. They survived by hunting and gathering, living a peaceful life in harmony with their environment. With the establishment of the Santa Clara Mission, the friars imposed a new life on the natives: a new religion, a new language, new survival skills including farming and raising cattle and, last but not least, new diseases. More natives were buried at the Santa Clara Mission than at any of the other missions.

SILICON VALLEY: *The History in Pictures*

PUEBLO SAN JOSE

Map of Downtown San Jose from 1886. Downtown San Jose developed around the initial pueblo which was near what is now the intersection of Highways 280 and 87. Library of Congress.

A Spanish frontier colony typically had three parts: the mission, the presidio and the pueblo. Missions were established to convert the native population; presidios were military forts; and pueblos were civil settlements tasked with providing food for the presidios. El Pueblo de San José was founded in 1777 a few months after Mission Santa Clara and the two institutions were located about three miles apart and connected by The Alameda. The Pueblo de San Jose was responsible for providing food and other supplies for the San Francisco and Monterey Presidios. The first census of the Pueblo of San Jose was in 1831 and totaled 524 inhabitants.

MEXICAN LAND GRANTS & THE RESULTING RANCHOS

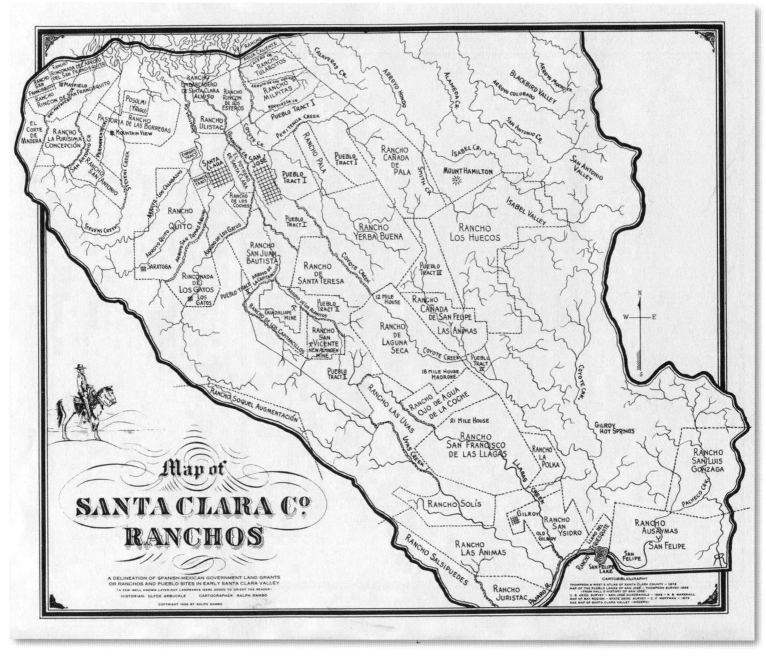

Map of Santa Clara County depicting the allocation of old Mission land to individual citizens granted by the Mexican Government upon their declaration of independence from Spain. Library of Congress.

The Jose Maria Alviso adobe house, built in 1837 and located in present day Milpitas, is now a historical monument as an example of the architecture from the days of the Ranchos.

In 1821 Mexico declared its independence from Spain and a California Assembly was created. The Assembly issued directives to put the land that was under control of the Spanish missions into secular hands. Under Mexican rule, the area was known as Alta California and the people who lived here were "Californios." The Santa Clara Mission claimed control of land from current day Palo Alto through Gilroy. In 1834 more than 800 ranchos were awarded in Santa Clara Valley ranging from a house lot up to 50,000 acres. Thus, most California rancheros became land barons to a greater or lessor degree. Authors have often referred to this period of history as the "Days of the Dons" and according to the Palo Alto Historical Association, "These rancho days were famed for beautiful senoritas, daring and handsome lovers, brave hunters, brutal sports and lavish hospitality." Many cities, neighborhoods and streets got their names from this era of history. Adobe architecture was the most prevalent during the rancho days. The photograph above is of an adobe house built in 1837 by Jose Maria Alviso who was an early alcalde (mayor) of the Pueblo de San Jose. The home is located in present day Milpitas and was built in the Monterey style which features a wood-shingled roof, wood balconies on three sides, French doors, interior fireplaces, and a symmetrical layout. The Alviso Adobe contains a remarkable amount of its original features; adobe walls from the 1830s, windows, doors and hardware from 1853 and an almost intact 1920s kitchen.

THE GOLD RUSH

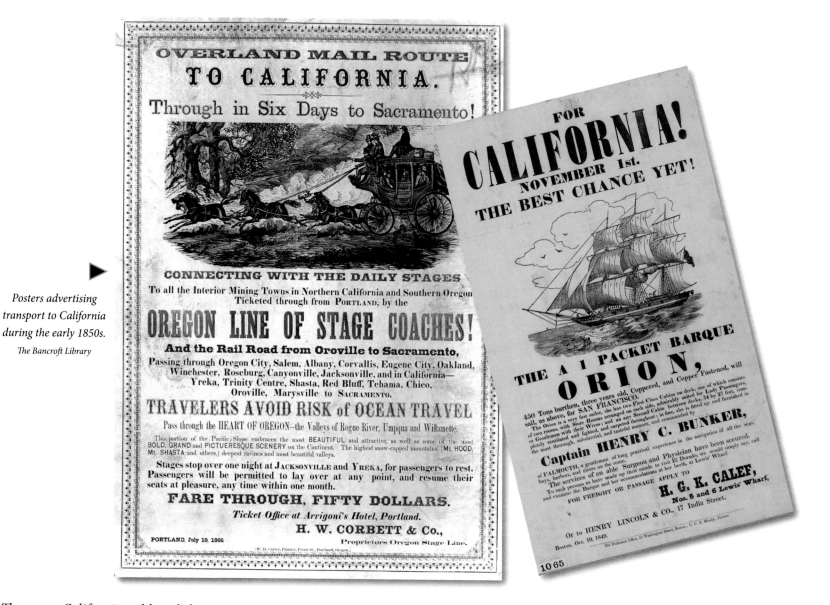

Posters advertising transport to California during the early 1850s.

The Bancroft Library

The great California gold rush began in 1848, when a gold nugget was discovered in the American River. News of the discovery brought thousands of immigrants to California from all over the world. At first, there were only two ways to travel out West. The first entailed a six month sea voyage from New York around the tip of South America to California, which brought with it rampant seasickness, bug infested food and a high price tag. The second route brought travelers in covered wagons over the rugged terrain and hostile territory of the Oregon-California Trail which also averaged six months. By 1850, the difficulty of both routes spurred construction of the Panama Railway, which shaved months off the voyage and helped foster continued immigration out west. The large influx of '49ers, as the gold prospectors were known, caused California's population to increase exponentially. Between 1848–1850, the population of San Francisco grew from 1,000 to over 20,000.

Uncomfortable conditions on the stage coach line prompted Wells Fargo to post the following rules for passenger behavior:

- *Abstinence from liquor is requested, but if you must drink share the bottle. To do otherwise makes you appear selfish and unneighborly.*

- *If ladies are present, gentlemen are urged to forgo smoking cigars and pipes as the odor of same is repugnant to the gentler sex.*

- *Chewing tobacco is permitted, but spit with the wind, not against it.*

- *Don't snore loudly while sleeping or use your fellow passenger's shoulder for a pillow.*

- *Firearms may be kept for use in emergencies. Do not fire them for pleasure or shoot at wild animals as the sound riles the horses.*

- *Forbidden topics of conversation include stagecoach robberies and Indian uprisings.*

San Jose Serves as the First State Capital

In 1899 San Jose built a replica of the first state capitol building as shown here, to mark the 50th anniversary of the event.

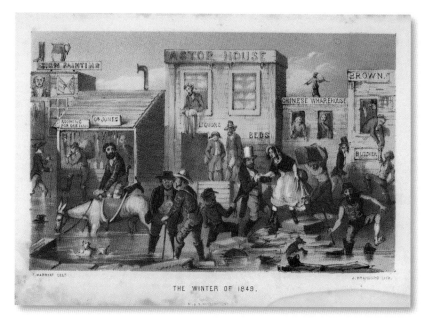

THE WINTER OF 1849.

A postcard depicting the wet and rather haphazard conditions the legislators found themselves in during the winter of 1849. The Bancroft Library.

In 1849 California's elected officials met in Monterey to draft a constitution in hopes that California would be admitted into the United States. After the people of California approved the new constitution it was sent to the United States Government. It took nearly a year for Congress to deliberate over the question of admitting California into the Union. Finally, and perhaps not coincidentally after gold had been discovered in California, President Fillmore signed the documents declaring California the 31st state. The first and second legislative sessions were held in San Jose in a two story adobe hotel, no more than 40 x 60 feet, during one of the wettest winters on record.

"Legislature of 1000 Drinks"

Palace Hotel Saloon, located at the corner of Cahill Street and The Alameda. Taken in 1902, it is one of the only remaining images of a bar during this era. According to San Jose historian, Leonard McKay, the second story of the saloon was a brothel.

It rained 36 inches the winter of 1849, well over twice the annual average for San Jose. The lawmakers complained about the accommodations and about the inclement weather and resorted to spending most of their time in the local saloons. Senator Green of Sacramento is credited for encouraging his fellow lawmakers with the slogan "Let's have a drink! Let's have a thousand drinks!" Due to the poor experience in San Jose, the capital was moved to Vallejo the following year and then permanently to Sacramento in 1854.

Cupertino Winery, 1891. California History Center.

Many who came West in the hopes of striking it rich in the gold fields soon found a better life was available to homesteaders who produced the necessities for California's burgeoning population. With its abundance of natural resources, fertile soil and temperate weather, Santa Clara Valley became the ideal spot for farmers, lumbermen and viticulturists. The abundant yield of the wheat crops grown in the fertile valley, the massive amounts of lumber produced in the Santa Cruz Mountains and the wine grapes that grew perfectly in the temperate climate of the foothills of the valley soon earned the area the title of "The Eden of the World."

TWO:
EARLY
INDUSTRIES

CALIFORNIA'S MAJESTIC REDWOODS

Reaching heights over 320 feet (the equivalent of a 30 floor skyscraper), California's state tree is in fact the world's tallest. The Coast Redwood can grow a trunk as wide as 24 feet and can live more than 2,000 years. The native population of California did not cut these trees down, but used fallen wood to build shelter and canoes. However, as hundreds of thousands of people flooded into California after the Gold Rush in 1850, the need for housing and timber grew exponentially and many looked to the Giant Redwood as the solution. Lumber from the Santa Cruz mountains became a hugely lucrative business for early Californians and the resulting deforestation went unregulated for the next 50 years.

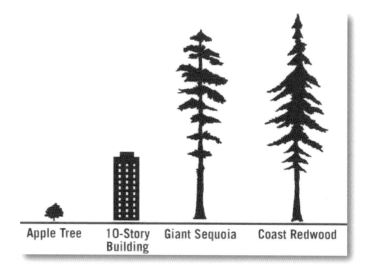

Apple Tree   10-Story Building   Giant Sequoia   Coast Redwood

Tourists posing within one of the giant redwoods in the Santa Cruz mountains circa 1880.
San Lorenzo Valley Museum.

LUMBERMEN

The lumbermen who arrived in the Santa Cruz mountains brought with them a long single blade called a whipsaw to cut the wood. The lumbermen would either dig a large pit or construct a sturdy platform where one man, the "pit-man," was positioned below the log and the "top-man" stood on top of the platform. The two-man team worked together to raise, lower, and guide the saw. The pit-man had to contend with sawdust in his mouth and eyes, not to mention the risk of being crushed by a falling log. While it was sometimes risky and the process tedious and the life lonely, many men found they could make more money splitting lumber than by working in the gold mines.

Whipsawers circa 1880.

Early lumbermen posing in the mountains circa 1880. San Lorenzo Valley Museum. ▶

LUMBER TRANSPORTATION

Oxen carrying the lumber down the mountainside, circa 1880. San Lorenzo Valley Museum.

Initially, lumbermen depended on longhorn oxen to carry the weight of the logs to the mills. The first step was to build a skid road which followed natural gullies downhill to the mill. They would bury logs every few feet in the skid road to help secure it and prevent unwanted mudslides. The final step was to smear beef tallow on each buried log, making it easier for the oxen to drag the cut logs down. Eight to ten yoke of oxen were used to pull a train of logs down the skid road to the mill.

South Pacific Coast Railway crossing over the Los Gatos Creek Trail, circa 1892. San Lorenzo Valley Museum.

Tunnel near Scotts Valley, circa 1892. San Lorenzo Valley Museum.

The introduction of the South Pacific Coast Railroad, which served the Santa Cruz Mountains beginning in the 1880s, made for faster and easier transportation of lumber. The newfound efficiency of the railroad coupled with the increased power of new mechanical logging methods caused lumber production to increase tenfold. In 1880 alone, Santa Cruz County generated ten million board feet of lumber.

LUMBER MILLS

One of the largest lumber mills at the time was the Pacific Manufacturing Company which was established in Santa Clara in 1874 and shortly thereafter became the largest wood product supplier on the Pacific Coast. Their lumber yard alone covered twenty acres and the mill warranted a private switch for the Southern Pacific Railroad. At the height of production the company employed up to 600 people. The business closed in 1960.

The Pacific Manufacturing plant was the largest industrial plant in the Valley, located in Santa Clara, circa 1898. Santa Clara City Library Heritage Pavilion. ▶

20

RESTORATION OF THE FORESTS

In 1899 San Jose photographer, Andrew P. Hill, was on assignment in the Santa Cruz Mountains to gather images of a fire in the redwoods that had been put out using wine from a local vineyard. The experience had a great effect on Hill and shortly thereafter, he began a quest to save the redwoods from deforestation. Hill convened a meeting with Stanford University's President, David Starr Jordan, as well as prominent scientists and other influential people to discuss what could be done to protect the redwoods. Out of this meeting came the Sempervirens Club whose mission was to lobby for the protection of the redwoods. After three years of campaigning, the efforts of the Sempervirens Club paid off. The state acquired 3,800 acres and created Big Basin Redwoods State Park, the first park established in California. Today, only 5% of the original redwoods remain and are all located in State Parks. This means that 95% of the redwood trees that currently exist today sprouted in the last 150 years after the deforestation of the late nineteenth century.

The first meeting of the Sempervirens Club in 1899. Sempervirens Club. ▶

Preservation acts by groups like the Sempervirens Club have helped restore much of the natural beauty to the California redwood forests as seen here.

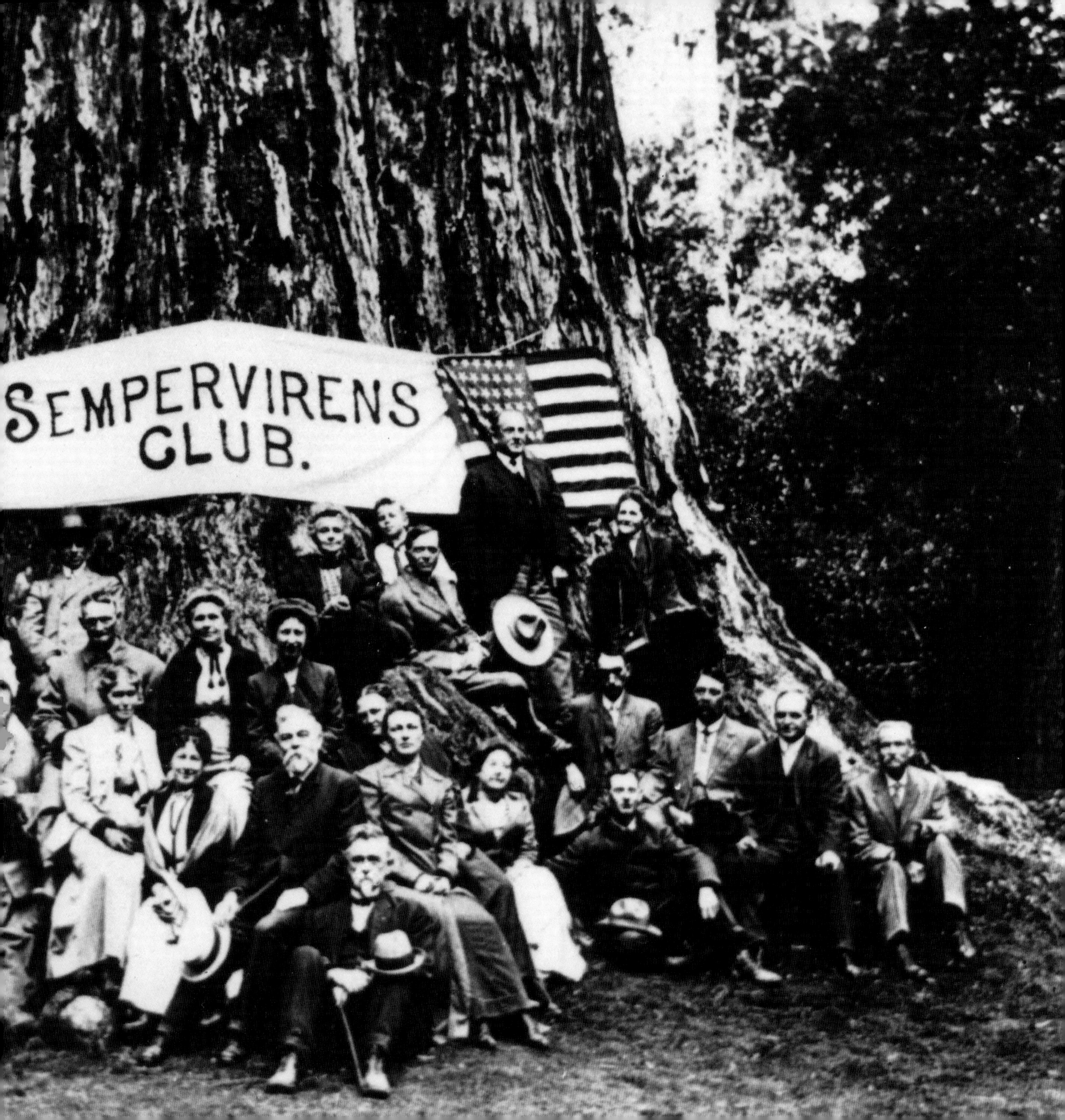
SEMPERVIRENS
CLUB.

GRAIN

Harvest time in 1910. Silicon Valley Historical Association.

Farmers bailing hay circa 1880. Silicon Valley Historical Association.

In the early 1850s farmers in the Santa Clara Valley realized that even without fertilizer, the land produced the best yields on wheat and barley they had ever seen. Thus began the period of commercial farming in the Valley. Wheat continued to be the dominant crop grown in the Valley from 1850–1880 and by 1868 the Santa Clara Valley was growing enough wheat to feed the entire state. During the Valley's wheat days, ranches sold for around $20 per acre. After orchards took over the landscape in the twentieth century, land was worth upwards of $400 per acre.

Farmers bailing hay circa 1890. Silicon Valley Historical Association.

Hay Stacks along the Alameda. California Room.

2863 – "The Old Stone Mill" – erected 1850. First Building in Los Gatos. California.

Postcard of Forbes Flour Mill in Los Gatos, circa 1905. California Room.

WINE

The history of wine-making and viticulture in the Santa Clara Valley goes back to the 18th Century when the padres at the Santa Clara Mission grew grapes for ceremonial wine. *Testarossa Winery.*

The Los Gatos Saratoga Wine and Fruit Company was built by local growers in 1885 to facilitate the processing of grapes. The winery was located on Saratoga-Los Gatos Road (Highway 9) in present day Monte Sereno. Saratoga Historical Foundation.

In 1852 Antoine Delmas imported his first European grapevines into the state. Eight years later, he also imported the first European winery and distillery equipment. Between 1849–1852 Santa Clara County attracted thousands of French and Italian settlers who immediately realized the potential of the valley and foothills for creating a world class wine district. At the time, wine was sold by the barrel to community grocery stores where customers simply brought their own bottles and filled them directly from the wine barrels. By 1870 the region's wines were consistently winning many awards.

WINE

In 1871 the president of Santa Clara University acquired acreage in the West Valley to produce wine for the school. Known as Villa Maria, this successful enterprise paved the way for the Jesuit Sacred Heart Novitiate and Winery in Los Gatos in the 1880s. Vincent Pichetti arrived from Italy in 1872 and managed the Villa Maria wine-making operation for more than a decade, later acquiring his own vineyard which is still around today. Each autumn from 1888 to 1986, the Jesuit winery harvested grapes. At one time, they picked enough fruit to produce 150,000 gallons of wine per year.

The Sacred Heart Novitiate in Los Gatos. Testarossa Winery. ▶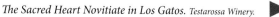

WINE: PROHIBITION

With the ratification of the Eighteenth Amendment to the United States Constitution in 1919, the era of Prohibition began and with it wiped out the burgeoning wine industry in Santa Clara Valley. Almost all of the wineries in California closed their doors between 1920 and 1933. Interesting to note however, is that during the period of Prohibition, people were still allowed to make wine at home for personal use. In fact, each male per household was allowed to produce 200 gallons of wine per year. Due to this rather interesting provision to the new law, the demand for California's wine grapes remained high. For this reason wine grape production remained consistent even as commercial wine-making all but disappeared. Wine began to flow again in the 1940s, and currently the Santa Cruz Mountains Winegrowers' Association boasts 48 member wineries. Most are small, family-owned operations and a number of them still have ties to the early wine-makers of the area.

The Sacred Heart Novitiate in Los Gatos after prohibition. Testarossa Winery.

BEER

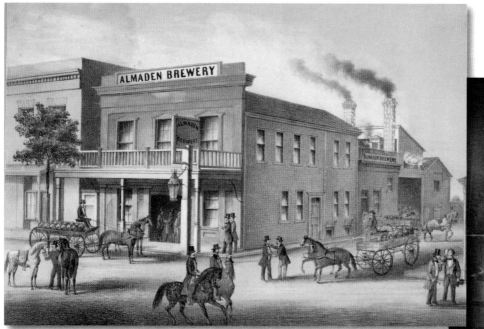

Almaden Brewery in San Jose, circa 1885. Bancroft Library.

The Santa Clara Brewery, photographed here in 1895, was owned by the German American Lauck family. It was located at the northeast corner of Benton and Alviso Streets. Santa Clara City Library.

Local beer making was another industry that arose from the arrival of the '49ers. There were a few notable characters who originally came west to make their fortunes in the gold mines but later returned to their known trade from back home. In 1853 the first brewery in the Santa Clara Valley was established and was named the Eagle Brewery. It was started by Joe Hartman in a shack on South Market Street in San Jose and in its humble beginnings, if a saloon needed a keg of beer, Joe put the keg in his wheelbarrow and delivered it himself. As business flourished, he moved to the corner of San Carlos and Market Streets and built the Eagle Brewery where the St. Claire Hotel stands today. The malt tower of the Eagle Brewery had six stories; making it the tallest building in San Jose at the time. In 1869 competition arrived when a German tavern keeper started the Fredericksburg Brewery on the corner of The Alameda and Cinnabar Street which is featured on the following spread. By the 1870s, a number of new breweries had popped up to accommodate the growing population. While the barley used was grown locally, the hops, bottles and barrels had to arrive by rail so most breweries were located on the railway.

Fredericksburg Brewery, 1884.

Fredericksburg Brewery, 1895.

The Fredericksburg Brewery opened in 1869 at the corner of The Alameda and Cinnabar Street by a German immigrant. It was one of the most popular businesses in the area until it closed in 1918. The following is a first-hand account of a brewery tour found in *Pen Pictures from the Garden of the World*, published by the Pacific Press Publishing Company in 1888:

"Embarking on one of the handsome cars of the Electric Road we are whirled rapidly along the famous Alameda Avenue, with its leafy shade, past the homes of wealthy men, sheltered with giant trees and embowered in flowers, to a point where stirring life and bustling activity proclaim the presence of some great enterprise. It is the Fredericksburg Brewery, the widest known and the most extensive establishment of its kind west of the Rocky Mountains."

Franklin Street in downtown Santa Clara in 1898. Santa Clara City Library Heritage Pavilion.

As logging and agriculture continued to flourish, towns began to spring up to support the growing population. The condition of affairs in San Jose around 1850 was described by Grandma Bascom who migrated to the area from Kansas. The following is an excerpt from *Overland Monthly and Out West Magazine*, May 1887:

Once in San Francisco we hoped to find a house which the Doctor had bought in New York and ordered sent around the Horn. He had also sent in the same cargo a great lot of furniture and a year's supply of provisions, but they didn't come until the next April and then everything was spoiled but the house...We always intended to come to the Santa Clara Valley, for the Doctor said that wherever the Catholic Fathers had picked out a site it must be a good one. The children and I stayed in the city while the Doctor went on horseback to San Jose and bought a house for us... We came to Alviso in the boat and paid $150 in fare, just for me and the children. From Alviso we came to San Jose by the Pioneer stage through fearful mud and pouring rain, paying an ounce (of gold) for each fare. (Once in San Jose), people began to ask if they could stay with us until they found some other home...The Legislature was in session and the town was more than full. Before I knew it, I had thirteen boarders—senators and representatives, ministers and teachers...In 1852 we moved out to our own farm in Santa Clara. I remember we paid our head carpenter $16 a day. The house cost us $10,000. It would not cost $1,000 now. An ounce of onion seed cost an ounce of gold. We paid $6 each for our fruit trees. A mule cost $300; a horse $400. But at the time, doctor's services were just as high-priced and so we kept even.

THREE:
EARLY TOWNS &
EARLY RESIDENTS

MAYFIELD

Mayfield's Main Street looking northwest from Sheridan Street, 1886. Palo Alto Historical Association.

The township of Mayfield was formed in 1855 and grew up around James Otterson's hotel, which opened in 1853 at the corner of El Camino Real and Lincoln Avenue (which is now known as California Avenue). Known as Uncle Jim's Cabin, it was patronized by travelers en route between San Francisco and San Jose and by lumbermen driving down from the hills. In the later part of the 19th century, Mayfield embodied the Wild West town spirit with over a dozen saloons and perhaps half as many brothels. However, by 1925 Mayfield decided to become part of Palo Alto due to economic considerations, which explains why Palo Alto has two downtown areas: one along University Avenue and one along California Avenue.

Uncle Jim's Cabin, a.k.a. the tavern of James Otterson, taken in 1874. Palo Alto Historical Association.

PALO ALTO

Looking down University Avenue in 1911 with an approaching street car. Silicon Valley Historical Association.

Postcard of El Palo Alto.

Looking down University Avenue in 1885. Silicon Valley Historical Association.

The city got its name from the tall landmark redwood tree, El Palo Alto, which still grows on the east bank of San Francisquito Creek across from Menlo Park. In 1886 Leland Stanford met with leaders of Mayfield to discuss his plans for the university and the need for a nearby town. He had one condition: alcohol had to be banned from the town. Known for its rowdy saloons, Mayfield rejected his requests for reform. This led Stanford to form a Temperance Town which he named Palo Alto. In 1894 Stanford purchased 740 acres from Timothy Hopkins (son of Railroad Barron, Mark Hopkins) to accommodate his new town and train station.

Los Altos

Downtown Los Altos, circa 1900. Los Altos History Museum.

In the 1800s, most of the acreage that is now Los Altos and Los Altos Hills was included in two Mexican land grants, Rancho la Purissima Concepcion and Rancho San Antonio. In the late 1800s, Sarah Winchester owned the 100 acres that later became the town site of Los Altos. In 1906 the Southern Pacific Railroad bought the land from Winchester for a right of way for their trains. Paul Shoup, who later became president of the Southern Pacific Railroad, helped create the town when he and others formed the Altos Land Company. The Shoup family built several summer homes along University Avenue that are still there today.

Map of the land purchased by the railroads from Sarah Winchester.

CUPERTINO

Cupertino Store in 1939 at the corner of Stevens Creek and Highway 9. California History Center.

The village of Cupertino sprang up at the crossroads of Highway 9 (now De Anza Boulevard) and Stevens Creek Road in the foothills of the valley. It was first known as West Side but by 1898 the post office at the crossroads needed a new name to distinguish it from other similarly named towns. John T. Doyle, a San Francisco lawyer and historian, had given the name Cupertino to his winery. In 1904 the name Cupertino caught on and was made official.

Postcard of the rolling foothills of Santa Clara County.

MOUNTAIN VIEW

Castro Street looking south. City of Mountain View.

In 1842 Francisco Estrada and his wife, Inez Castro were granted the 8,800 acre Rancho Pastoria de las Borregas. In 1850 a Stage Coach stop was established near Grant Road and El Camino Real. Naturally, the initial commercial hub of Mountain View developed in this area. In the 1860s, Henry Rengstorff built docks, wharves and warehouses near present day Shoreline Amphitheatre to ship the region's agricultural products to San Francisco. The San Francisco and San Jose Railroad was completed in 1864 and placed a depot on Evelyn Avenue, which shifted the downtown area from Grant Road to Castro Street.

Postcard of the oak trees that were scattered along the valley floor.

Alviso

The Alviso Hotel in 1905. California Room.

In 1840 Ignacio Alviso moved south from Mission Santa Clara to the Rancho Rincon de Los Esteros, meaning corner of the estuaries. The town that bears his name was once a thriving port, which offered merchants a way to transport their beaver pelts, cattle hides and tallow by ship to San Francisco. Alviso was instrumental in establishing both the port and a fine hotel pictured here. Some buildings from that era still exist today.

The Alviso Regatta during its heyday. South Bay Yacht Club.

SARATOGA

Saratoga post office circa 1894. Saratoga Historical Society.

Saratoga derived its name in the 1850s from the discovery of mineral springs, which had a chemical content similar to the great Saratoga Springs in New York. The first acknowledged permanent American settler in Saratoga was William Campbell who started a sawmill operation in 1847. Saratoga soon became a stagecoach stop between the Santa Cruz Mountains and the valley floor. Hotels and saloons were strung out along Lumber Street (now Big Basin Way) and a rough frontier atmosphere prevailed as late as the 1880s.

Postcard of the Saratoga Foothills.

SUNNYVALE

Murphy Avenue in Downtown Sunnyvale, circa 1915. Sunnyvale Historical Society.

Sunnyvale was originally named after Martin Murphy Jr. who was the first prominent resident in the area. In 1860 Murphy allowed The San Francisco and San Jose Railroad to establish Murphy Station and later Lawrence Station on his property. In 1901 the residents of Murphy were informed that they could not use the name Murphy for their post office and decided to use the name Sunnyvale, not just for the post office but for the name of their town as well.

Murphy Avenue businesses circa 1908. Sunnyvale Historical Society.

LOS GATOS

Main Street in Los Gatos looking east circa 1908. Looking closely, you can see a gato crossing in front of the stagecoach. Saratoga Historical Society.

Postcard of Los Gatos, circa 1910.

Los Gatos received its name due to the many mountain lions that came to drink from the Los Gatos Creek. In 1854 James Alexander Forbes purchased some land on the Los Gatos Creek and built a flour mill, which became the nucleus around which the town of Los Gatos was built. Los Gatos became a desired place for city dwellers to build a second summer home, as well as a resting spot for railroad passengers traveling between San Francisco and Santa Cruz.

Lexington / Alma

Alma Train Station, circa 1925.

The Alma Country Store.

1915 Alma view across the meadow towards the country store.

Train station in Alma, circa 1925.

In 1860 an immigrant from Kentucky bought some property at the base of the Santa Cruz Mountains and named it Lexington after his home town. This little outpost became a stop on the stagecoach route from Los Gatos to Santa Cruz. The local base of influence transferred from Lexington to another outpost nearby named Alma, when in 1880, the narrow gauge railway from Alviso to Santa Cruz went through Alma instead of Lexington. Folklore says the town of Alma was named after a local prostitute. Alma had a hotel, saloons and a general merchandise store. Following the completion of State Route 17, the railroad ceased operations in 1940 and the area fell into a period of decline. In 1952 the Lexington Reservoir was created and both Lexington and Alma were officially abandoned. Old roads and building foundations from these frontier towns are often visible under Lexington Reservoir during periods of low water level.

SANTA CLARA

Franklin Street in downtown Santa Clara in 1898. Santa Clara City Library Heritage Pavilion.

In the 1850s Santa Clara began to take shape as a recognizable small town. The town site was surveyed by William Campbell into lots of one hundred square yards. One lot was given to each citizen with the understanding that he was to build a house on it within three months or lose the property. A schoolhouse and a church were built; several hotels erected; mercantile businesses established; and 23 houses were imported from Boston to be set up in the town. In 1851 Santa Clara University was established on the old mission site and became a prominent feature of the developing town. Two of the earliest manufacturing businesses in Santa Clara were the Wampach Tannery, established in 1849, and the Pacific Manufacturing Company, established in 1874.

SAN JOSE

Downtown San Jose in 1908. *History San Jose.*

Postcard of Downtown San Jose from 1920.

Postcard of Downtown San Jose in 1896. This view is looking north down market street with St. Joseph Church on the right.

In 1775 Juan Bautista de Anza led the first overland expedition to bring colonists from New Spain (Mexico) to Alta California to prepare for two missions, one presidio (military fort), and one pueblo (town). The site of the pueblo was initially located near the present-day intersection of Guadalupe Parkway and Taylor Street and was designed as a farming community to serve the presidios of San Francisco and Monterey. In 1797 the pueblo was moved from its original location to what is now Plaza de César Chávez in downtown San Jose. In 1881 San Jose installed a 237 foot electrified tower as an alternative to lighting the city with gas. The experiment didn't go as planned but the tower remained operational for years as an attraction to be lit up on holidays and festivals. See postcard lower right.

MARTIN MURPHY JR.

The Murphy House. Sunnyvale Historical Society.

Martin Murphy Jr. was part of the Stephens-Townsend-Murphy Party, famous for being the first wagon party to cross the Sierras which they accomplished in 1844. In 1850 Martin Murphy Jr. purchased 4,800 acres in what is now Sunnyvale and Mountain View for about $1 an acre and soon became the most wealthy man in California. The Murphy residence as seen above was a clapboard house built in Maine, disassembled, shipped around Cape Horn to Sunnyvale and then reassembled. In 1881 Martin Murphy Jr. celebrated his golden wedding anniversary and invited the entire state of California. Attendance to the party was estimated to be between 10,000 - 15,000 people.

James Lick

The Lick Observatory. *California Room.*

Born in Pennsylvania in 1796, James Lick learned the art of piano making at an early age. At 25 he discovered that his pianos were being exported to South America. He decided to move there and spent some years in a number of countries in South America. In 1846 he moved to San Francisco and immediately began buying up real estate in San Francisco as well as large tracts of undeveloped land further south. He built the largest flour mill in the state and with the discovery of gold shortly thereafter, Lick made his fortune by catering to the population boom. Prior to his death in 1876 Lick was the richest man in California. He designated a large portion of his fortune be used to establish a mountain top observatory to house the largest and most powerful telescope yet built by man. The site was selected to be on the summit of Mount Hamilton, in the eastern San Jose foothills. The observatory still exists today.

MOUNTAIN CHARLIE

A painting of Mountain Charlie done in 1894. History San Jose

Charles McKiernan was born in Ireland in 1825 and came to San Francisco in 1848 in the hopes of finding gold. Upon his arrival, he discovered wages were $20 per day as opposed to the $20 per year he could make in Ireland. After accumulating a nice savings, he headed down to the Santa Cruz Mountains and established his homestead where Redwood Estates now joins Summit Road. He lived in the mountains completely alone for three years. He raised long-horned steers and hunted deer and would ship his animal products to San Francisco via ferry from Alviso. At the time, there were no roads in the mountains so McKiernan built several, one of which still bears his name. He became a local legend after a bear attack that crushed the front of his skull and left him terribly disfigured. He died in 1892, 38 years after the attack.

SARAH WINCHESTER

The Winchester House before the 1906 Earthquake when it stood seven stories tall. California Room.

Sarah grew up in New Haven and married William Winchester in 1862. Their only daughter died as an infant and 15 years later her husband died of Tuberculosis. The deaths devastated Sarah and left her the sole heir to her husband's $20 million estate. In 1892 she moved to San Jose and purchased an eight room house on 150 acres. Folklore says that Sarah continued to build onto the house as a way to appease the many spirits who were killed by Winchester rifles. When Sarah passed away in 1922 her Victorian house was seven stories tall and contained 160 rooms, with 47 fireplaces, 10,000 window panes, 17 chimneys and three elevators. The house is now a historic monument and provides daily tours.

South Pacific Coast Railway in the Santa Cruz Mountains, circa 1892. San Lorenzo Valley Museum.

Prior to 1850, to get from San Francisco to San Jose, the only mode of transportation was via stagecoach using an old French omnibus pulled by a mule. The trip took nine hours and cost two ounces of gold or $32.00. With the large influx of immigrants and the economic vibrancy of the area, large investments were made to install more modern modes of transportation. Two railways were built, the first from San Francisco to San Jose, with a later branch covering the West Valley via Los Altos. The second railroad was a narrow gage railway and stretched from Santa Cruz to Alviso. By 1896 there were 15 daily trains from San Jose to San Francisco, which cost the rider $1.25 each way. Furthermore, the port of Alviso was a major hub of commerce as ships would travel up and down the bay carrying passengers and freight. Lastly, there was the Peninsular Interurban, which was a hybrid between a railroad and a city trolley car. The Interurban was headquartered in San Jose and connected Palo Alto in the north, Saratoga in the west, Los Gatos in the south and Alum Rock Park in the east, with stops in San Jose and Santa Clara. One could board a car in say, Saratoga, and travel to Stanford for a football game or a day of shopping and appointments in downtown San Jose, as service was every half-hour. It was a true modern metro network that, due to corporate greed and lack of foresight by the local government during the 1940s and 50s, is now a luxury that the residents of Santa Clara County only dream about.

FOUR:
EARLY
TRANSPORTATION

THE SAN FRANCISCO & SAN JOSE RAILROAD

After California gained statehood in 1850, there was increased need for travel between San Francisco and San Jose. The San Francisco and San Jose Railroad was built between 1861 and 1864. Upon completion, the line was 49.5 miles long and the trip took 2 hours and 20 minutes. The San Francisco and San Jose Railroad was acquired by The Southern Pacific Railroad in 1868.

Santa Clara railroad station, at the corner of Benton Street and Railroad Avenue, circa 1900. Santa Clara City Library Heritage Pavilion. ▶

San Francisco and San Jose Railroad

SAN FRANCISCO AND SAN JOSE RAILROAD.

TIME TABLE

For the government and information of employes only. It is not intended for the information of the public, the Company reserving the right to vary therefrom as circumstances may require.

TAKES EFFECT AUGUST 1ST, 1866.

NORTHWARD TRAINS.											SOUTHWARD TRAINS.						
SUNDAYS.			WEEK DAYS.				Distance from San Jose.	NAMES OF STATIONS AND PASSING PLACES.		Distance from San Francisco.	WEEK DAYS.				SUNDAYS.		
EVE.	EVE.	MOR.	FRT.	EVE.	MOR.	MOR.					MOR.	EVE.	EVE.	FRT.	MOR.	MOR.	EVE.
9.50	6.10	10.30	11.30	6.10	9.30	8.30	49¾	Ar. San Francisco,	Dep.		8.20	4.30	5.30	12.30	8.30	9.50	4.10
9.45	6.05	10.25		6.05	9.25	**8.25**	46¼	" * Mission,	"	3½	**8.25**	4.35	5.35		8.35	9.55	4.15
9.40	6.00	10.20		6.00	9.20	8.20	45½	" * Bernal,	"	4¼	8.30	4.40	5.40		8.40	10.00	4.20
9.30	5.50	**10.10**	10.50	**5.50**	9.10	8.10	43½	" * San Miguel,	"	6¼	8.40	4.50	**5.50**		8.50	**10.10**	4.30
9.23	5.43	10.03		5.43	9.03	8.03	40¾	" * School House,	"	9	8.47	4.57	5.57		8.57	10.17	4.37
9.16	5.36	9.56		5.36	**8.56**	7.56	38¼	" * 12 Mile Farm,	"	11½	**8.56**	5.06	6.06		9.06	10.26	4.46
9.09	5.29	9.49		5.29	8.49	7.49	35½	" * San Bruno,	"	14¼	9.01	5.11	6.11		9.11	10.31	4.51
9.00	5.20	9.40		**5.20**	8.40	7.40	33	" Millbrae,	"	16¾	9.10	**5.20**	6.20	2.00	9.23	10.40	5.00
8.50	**5.10**	**9.30**	9.25	5.10	8.30	7.30	29	" San Mateo,	"	20¾	9.20	5.30	6.30	2.20	**9.30**	10.50	**5.10**
8.37	4.57	9.17	9.10	4.57	8.17	7.17	24¾	" Belmont,	"	25	9.33	5.43	6.43	2.35	9.43	11.03	5.23
8.30	4.50	9.10	8.50	4.50	8.10	7.10	21½	" Redwood City,	"	28¼	9.40	5.50	6.50	2.50	9.50	11.10	5.30
8.20	4.40	9.00	8.20	4.40	8.00	6.55	17¼	" Menlo Park,	"	32½	9.50	6.00	7.00	3.15	10.00	11.20	5.40
8.13	4.33	8.53	8.10	4.33	7.53	6.50	15¼	" Mayfield,	"	34½	9.57	6.07	7.10	3.30	10.07	11.27	5.47
8.02	4.22	8.42	7.45	4.22	7.42		9¾	" Mountain View,	"	40	10.08	6.18		4.00	10.18	11.38	5.58
7.48	4.08	8.28	7.27	4.08	7.28		6	" Lawrence's,	"	43¾	10.22	6.32		4.20	10.32	11.52	6.12
7.40	4.00	8.20	7.15	4.00	7.20		3¼	" Santa Clara,	"	46½	10.30	6.40		4.35	10.40	12.00	6.20
7.30	3.50	8.10	7.00	3.50	7.10			Dep. San Jose,	Ar.	49¾	10.40	6.50		5.00	10.50	12.10	6.30

☞ * Indicates Flag Stations.

☞ 1. The figures set against San Francisco Northward, and San Jose Southward, are the times to REACH those Stations. The other figures represent the times of LEAVING the Stations against which they are placed.

☞ 2. The figures in large black type designate the meeting places of trains, and the time of passing.

☞ 3. In case freight train is not at passing place on time, passenger train will proceed with caution until such train is passed.

☞ 4. Freight train must keep clear of all regular passenger trains at least ten minutes.

☞ 5. All irregular trains must keep clear of regular trains at least fifteen minutes.

☞ 6. Freight train leaving San Jose at 7.00, P. M., will wait the arrival of the 4.30, P. M., train from San Francisco.

☞ 7. The 7.00, P. M., freight from San Jose must not pass Mayfield until the 5.30, P. M., train from San Francisco arrives.

☞ 8. Should freight train leaving San Francisco at 12.30, A. M., be delayed it must keep clear of trains leaving Mayfield at 6.50, A. M., and San Jose at 7.10, A. M.

☞ 9. **All Regular Passenger Trains will wait twenty (20) minutes at passing places designated in the Time Table, and then proceed, always keeping twenty (20) minutes behind Card time until the expected train is passed. When both trains lose the twenty (20) minutes, they will proceed with flag in advance, and run with caution until trains pass.** See General Rules, No. 24.

☞ 10. **San Francisco and San Jose are terminal stations. All regular passenger trains will leave terminal stations on time, notwithstanding trains may be due. A train loses its right of road which does not reach the terminus before the starting time of a regular train. No excuse will be received for neglect of any of these rules.**

Oct. 31. st. 192

1923

CHAS. B. GOULD, Acting Superintendent.

Railroad time table from 1866. South Bay Historical Railroad Society.

Menlo Park Train Station, looking towards Palo Alto, 1885. Palo Alto Historical Association.

The train leaving the Palo Alto station and steaming towards the famous El Palo Alto tree in 1894. Palo Alto Historical Association.

SAN FRANCISCO AND SAN JOSE RAILROAD

3510 The Southern Pacific Broad Gauge Depot, San Jose, California.

Postcard of the Southern Pacific Railroad station in San Jose, 1911. California Room.

In 1908 Southern Pacific Railroad began running steam train service through Los Altos with 5 trains per day. This was a secondary Southern Pacific route that passed through the Stanford University campus in Palo Alto. It was abandoned in 1962 to make way for the Foothill Expressway. Image taken in Palo Alto. Los Altos Historical Society.

Murphy Station railroad stop in Sunnyvale, looking east circa 1911. Sunnyvale Historical Society.

THE PACIFIC COAST RAILWAY

A restored train from the early 1900s currently serving tourists visiting the Santa Cruz mountains.

Originally known as The Santa Clara Valley Railroad, the South Pacific Coast Railway was a narrow gauge railway that was constructed to serve the lumbermen and fruit growers as shipping prices became cost prohibitive on the San Francisco–San Jose Railroad. It was built in two sections: the first from the port in Newark to Los Gatos, with stops in Santa Clara and Alviso; and the second from Los Gatos to Santa Cruz. The full train track was 45 miles long and opened in 1880. The invention of the refrigerated railroad car in the late 1800s allowed the Valley to become the largest fruit production and packing region in the world as this allowed them to ship large quantities of perishable goods and keep them fresh during transport.

Loading a refrigerated train cabin, 1890.
Silicon Valley Historical Association.

The Pacific Coast Railway, steaming past the Santa Cruz Beach Boardwalk.

Advertisement for Casa del Rey, a casino and resort on the Santa Cruz beach.

While initially set up as a freight service, tourism from San Francisco to the beaches in Santa Cruz became a popular service and special trains were set up to cater to the weekend revelers. This train service was called the Suntan Special and a round trip ticket cost $1.25. Resorts sprung up throughout the mountains and along the beach in Santa Cruz to cater to the new influx of tourists.

Postcard of the Santa Cruz Beach Boardwalk from its heyday.

THE ALVISO REGATTA

Before train service, the most efficient way to get from the Valley to San Francisco was to take a boat from Alviso, which cost $35. After passengers migrated to the San Francisco–San Jose Railway in 1864, Alviso remained a popular trading post for merchants. This small port town became even more important after the introduction of the Pacific Coast Railway that brought lumber and fruit by rail to Alviso to be placed on a steamship bound for San Francisco. The narrow gage railway that served the port of Alviso was abandoned in 1942 which led to the town's ultimate demise.

Steamboat landing in Alviso, 1895. San Jose History Center.

The Alviso Regatta in 1912. The South Bay Yacht Club in the background was built in 1903 and still serves as the club's headquarters today. California Room.

INTERURBAN TRANSPORTATION

1907 Streetcar in Los Gatos. Santa Clara City Library Heritage Pavilion.

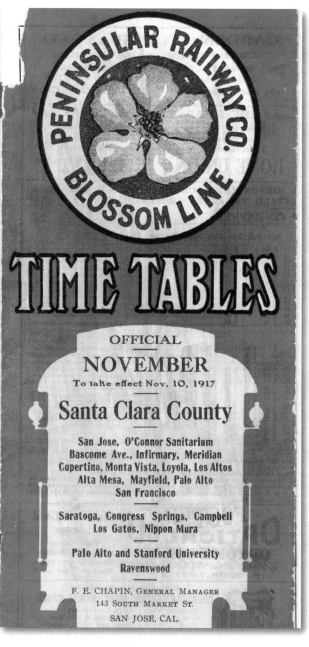

1917 timetable. California History Center.

1915 Streetcar on Santa Cruz Avenue in Los Gatos. California History Center.

San Jose was the first city in California to have a streetcar, which was introduced in 1890. Trolley lines eventually covered 70 miles of track and many lines provided train service every seven minutes between the downtown San Jose core and then outlying towns including Santa Clara, Monta Vista, Los Altos, Los Gatos, Alum Rock, and Beryessa, as well as further out to Palo Alto and Stanford. In 1920 streetcar trains reached the center of San Jose from the far points of the line in about 15–20 minutes. Around the same time, there were more than 30,000 streetcars in the United States, using approximately 15,000 miles of track and carrying more than 11 billion passengers a year. These electric streetcars ran on tracks and used a pole to draw power from an overhead wire.

1937 streetcar traveling eastbound on The Alameda at Newhall Street in San Jose.

In 1938 bus service replaced all electric streetcars due to a push by corporate America to get Americans in cars.

Yet only a few decades later these streetcars were abandoned; the last streetcar service in San Jose was in 1938. The replacement of streetcars with buses across the country is known as The Great American Streetcar Scandal. General Motors, Firestone Tire, Standard Oil of California, Phillips Petroleum, Mack Trucks, and the Federal Engineering Corporation have been accused of buying over 100 electric surface-traction systems in 45 cities across the country and converting them into bus operation to further their corporate interests and push the US into automobile dependency. The story has been explored several times in print, film and other media, notably in the movies Who Framed Roger Rabbit, Taken for a Ride and The End of Suburbia.

Palm Drive into Stanford University, 1891. Stanford University Archives.

FIVE: STANFORD UNIVERSITY

THE STANFORD FAMILY

Stanford farm home in Palo Alto circa 1887. Stanford University Archives.

Leland Stanford, who grew up and studied law in New York, moved west to chase the gold rush and ended up making his fortune in the railroad that followed. He was a leader of the Republican Party, Governor of California and later a U.S. Senator. He and Jane had one son who died of typhoid fever in 1884 when the family was traveling in Italy. Leland Jr. was just 15. Within weeks of his death, the Stanfords decided that, because they no longer could do anything for their own child, "The children of California shall be our children." They quickly set about to find a lasting way to memorialize their beloved son.

Stanford family photo taken in 1881. Stanford University Archives.

The Harvard of the West

Middlefield Road in 1890. Silicon Valley Historical Association.

Stanford University Postcard. Stanford University Archives.

Leland Stanford acquired more than 8,000 acres of adjoining properties to house his new university. The Stanfords engaged Frederick Law Olmsted, the famed landscape architect who created New York's Central Park, to design the physical plan for the university. On October 1, 1891 Stanford University opened its doors after six years of planning and building. The first student body consisted of 555 men and women, and the original faculty of 15 was expanded to 49 for the second year.

Stanford students in the 1920s. Stanford University Archives.

Did You Know?

If companies founded by Stanford graduates formed an independent nation, it would be the 10th largest economy in the world. California is home to about 18,000 firms created by Stanford alumni, generating annual worldwide sales of about $1.27 trillion and employing more than three million people. Conducted in 2011, the study entitled *Stanford University's Economic Impact via Innovation and Entrepreneurship* analyzed the results of a large survey of Stanford alumni and faculty. The findings were published by Charles Eesley, an assistant professor in the Stanford School of Engineering, and computer scientist William F. Miller of the Stanford Graduate School of Business.

HERBERT HOOVER

Herbert Hoover campaigning for President in Palo Alto in 1928. Stanford University Archives.

Herbert Hoover entered Stanford University in 1891, its inaugural year, after flunking all the entrance exams (except mathematics) and then being tutored for the summer in Palo Alto. Hoover claimed to be the very first student at Stanford, by virtue of being the first person in the first class to sleep in the dormitory. While at the university, he was a part of the inaugural Big Game versus rival University of California (Stanford won).

SILICON VALLEY: *The History in Pictures*

Hoover Tower in 1939. Stanford University Archives.

Hoover Tower in 1941. Stanford University Archives.

Hoover Tower, inspired by the cathedral tower at Salamanca, was built to commemorate Stanford's 50th anniversary. It was finished in 1941, stands 285 feet tall and houses the Hoover Institution Library and Archives. Hoover had amassed a large collection of materials related to early 20th century history and donated them to Stanford prior to becoming president.

Farm land in Santa Clara Valley in the 1930s. Silicon Valley Historical Association.

Towards the end of the 1800s, farmers realized that fruit and nuts grew very well in the temperate valley. Because the return on investment in an orchard was so much higher than a grain field, land values started to rise. According to the book published in 1896 entitled *Sunshine, Fruit and Flowers,* land that once produced grain and cost $15 per acre, now commanded $200–$600 per acre for the most suitable plots for fruit orchards. While everything from cherries to pears, berries, almonds, apricots, apples and tomatoes fared extremely well in the valley, it was the prune that was the most profitable, and therefore the most extensive crop. Around this time, over 200 million pounds of fresh, dried and canned fruit was exported from the valley every year. There was no better place on earth to grow fruit than Santa Clara Valley, and soon the area became known as "The Valley of Heart's Delight."

Six:
Valley of Heart's Delight

ORCHARDS

Apricot Drying Racks in the Valley circa 1936. Silicon Valley Historical Association.

In the 1870s wheat farming in Santa Clara County became uneconomical due to soil degradation and new county property tax laws. Small fruit orchards replaced the large wheat farms and farmers branched out into a wide array of crops: prunes, apricots, peaches, pears, cherries, oranges, almonds, walnuts.

Farm land in Santa Clara Valley in the 1930s. Silicon Valley Historical Association.

In 1919 there were nearly 100,000 acres of fruit trees, 3,000 acres of wine grapes, and 85,000 acres of grains, vegetables and berries. In that same year, the farmers in Santa Clara County received $45 million from the products of their trees (equivalent to $590 million in today's dollars). The crop was by far the largest ever raised in the Santa Clara Valley.

FRUIT PACKING, CANNING & DRYING

A fruit processing center in the 1950s. Silicon Valley Historical Association.

In 1871 the first cannery, box and fruit packing companies opened in Santa Clara Valley. The development of food processing technology, including canning and drying, created a new opportunity for growers in Santa Clara Valley. During the heyday, the canneries in Santa Clara Valley shipped ten million cans of fruit and vegetables worldwide annually. During the canning season, the air would be filled with the fragrance of cherries, plums, tomatoes, and other fruits being processed. In 1917 when the U.S. entered World War I, the canneries enjoyed an increased demand for canned fruit to feed the soldiers. In addition, the lack of a male work force due to the draft created new opportunities for women to enter the workforce.

Workers on an assembly line at the Ferry-Morse Seed Co. in Mountain View in 1960. City of Mountain View.

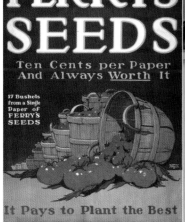

Ferry–Morse Seed Co. started in Mountain View in the 1870s and grew to be the largest seed producer in the world. At harvest time, the company employed 500 people. Ferry-Morse Seed Co. was located in a triangular parcel of land bounded by Mountain View–Alviso Road (now Highway 237), Whisman Road and Evelyn Avenue. In 1985 the plant closed and moved to Modesto and shortly thereafter Hewlett Packard moved into the former Ferry–Morse site.

FRUIT PACKING, CANNING & DRYING

Sunsweet Packing Plant in Campbell.

By 1960 there were 215 fruit processing operations in the Valley. Not only was fruit processing the largest employer, it provided a market for many other local industries including: label makers, fruit box makers, can makers, machinery providers and shippers. Restaurants and bars also cropped up near the processing plants to cater to the fruit workers.

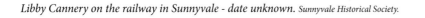

Libby Cannery on the railway in Sunnyvale - date unknown. Sunnyvale Historical Society.

Libby Cannery opened its doors in Sunnyvale in 1909. At the time, workers received about $1.50–$3.75 per day at piece rate; in today's dollars that would be a daily wage of $35–$95. By 1922 Libby's was the largest cannery in the world. Like the Libby Cannery noted here, most canneries and fruit packers located themselves along the rail line for easy transportation of their canned goods.

Libby's

FANCY QUALITY

FANCY FRUITS FOR SALAD

BLOSSOM TOURS

Postcard of a field of sweet peas near San Jose, circa 1908. California History Center.

Postcard of blooming orchards in Los Gatos, circa 1911. California History Center.

1953 tour map showing when the best viewing times were for each type of orchard. The Santa Clara City Library Heritage Pavilion.

BLOSSOMTIME TOURS

SANTA CLARA VALLEY
BLOSSOM ROUTES

MORNING TOUR

AFTERNOON TOUR

ALTERNATE ROUTES

Copyright by:
The H. M. Gousha Company

Blossom Dates . . .

ALMONDS: Jan. 15 to Feb. 15   **APRICOTS:** Feb. 23 to Mar. 1

PRUNES: Mar. 15 to Mar. 22   **PEARS:** Mar. 15 to Mar. 22   **CHERRIES:** Mar. 22 to April 5

The above dates indicate approximately when the largest number of blossoms may be expected to be found on each particular variety of tree although weather conditions may cause dates to vary somewhat.

GREATER SAN JOSE CHAMBER OF COMMERCE

STREET CLOSED

MARIN ROCK CO. CONTRACTORS.

RA... IMPROVE...

Paving of Highway 9 in 1915. The Cupertino Store is at the right. California History Center.

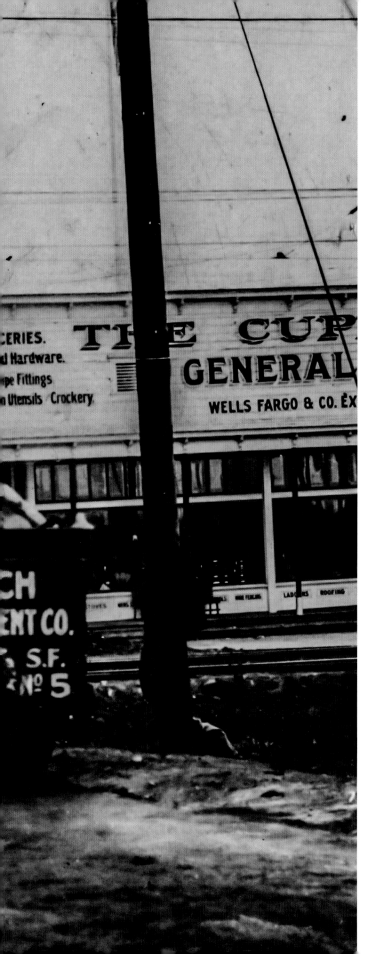

Jim Nissen and a friend in 1950. Nissen was the grandfather of the San Jose Airport. In 1945 he opened "California Aviation Activities" and built the first dirt runway where the airport stands today. San Jose Airport Commission.

The beginning of the 20th century saw the introduction of the personal automobile and half a century later, air transportation. One of the most visible changes resulting from the personal automobile was the replacement of train tracks with freeways. For example, in 1959 the railway tracks that once served the Santa Cruz mountains were torn out to make way for Highway 17. In 1962 Foothill Expressway was built upon the right of way that previously served as the tracks for the Los Altos branch of the Peninsular Railway. The buildings at Loyola Corners in South Los Altos are historical railroad station buildings. In 1949 the first commercial air flight landed in San Jose which ushered in the era of air transportation for Valley residents.

SEVEN:
A TRANSPORTATION
TRANSFORMATION

INTRODUCTION OF THE PERSONAL AUTOMOBILE

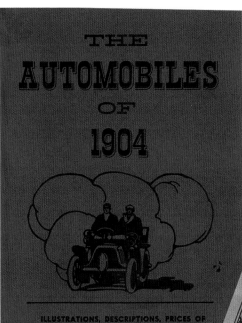

A horseless carriage circa 1910 in Palo Alto. Silicon Valley Historical Association.

The large-scale assembly line manufacturing of affordable automobiles was greatly expanded by Henry Ford in the early 1900s. Ford's cars came off the line in fifteen minute intervals, increasing productivity 800% while using less manpower. His process was so successful that by 1914 an assembly line worker could buy a Model T with four month's pay.

Downtown Santa Clara in 1920. Silicon Valley Historical Association.

Wine delivery via car, 1920.

City of Mountain View.

The traffic jam begins! El Camino Real in 1940. Hoover Tower is in the background. Palo Alto Historical Association.

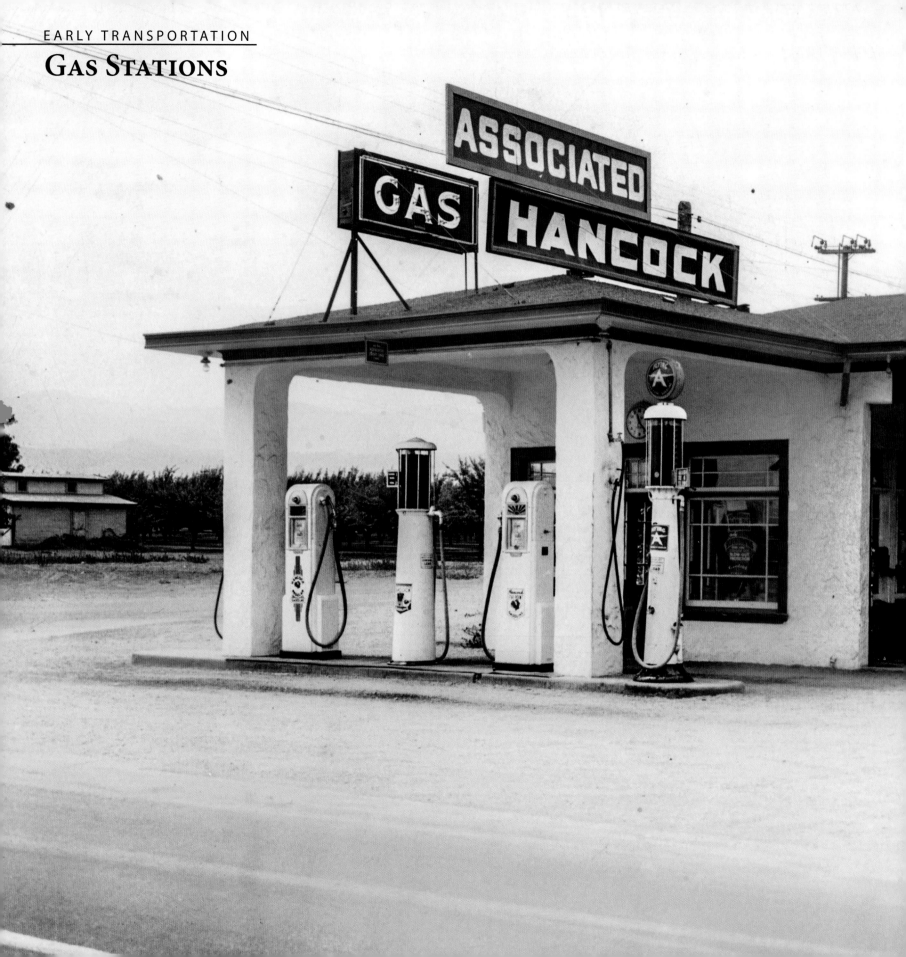

Charlie Baer's gas station in Cupertino circa 1935. In 1922 Charlie ripped down his father's old Blacksmith shop and Cupertino's first auto service station replaced it. This site was on the northwest corner of Stevens Creek Road and De Anza Boulevard —a bank currently sits in that location. *California History Center.*

THE AGE OF THE FREEWAY

Highway 17 in 1960. Ruins of Forbes Mill can be seen on the right. The California Room.

Once cars became the main mode of transportation, the era of the freeway commenced. Highway 101 was commissioned in 1926 as one of the original US highways extending from the Mexican border to Washington State. The portion of the freeway between San Jose and San Francisco was a four lane road with no median and was known as Bloody Bayshore due to the high frequency of accidents. Between 1949 and 1962 the road was upgraded to between six and ten lanes. Interstate 280 was added to the Interstate Highway System in 1955 as an additional route between San Jose and San Francisco. However, the freeway was not completed until the 1970s. In 1959 Highway 17 opened up between Los Gatos and San Jose roughly following the former Pacific Coast Railway.

Highway 101 in 1940.

Highway 280 in 1970. Silicon Valley Historical Association.

SAN JOSE AIRPORT

"Airport Day" - The 1945 inaugural flight into San Jose drew crowds to witness the landing along with the newly constructed runway and terminal building. San Jose Airport Authority.

The San Jose International Airport had its birth in the declining years of the Great Depression, when San Jose had a population of less than 68,000 and its economy was linked to the thousands of acres of orchards that stretched out from its city limits. Aviation enthusiasm had been growing since the early 1920s when World War I fly boys returned to put on exhibitions and conduct flying schools. In 1945 Jim Nissen leased 16 acres of land in San Jose for a small aviation business, California Aviation Activities, and built the first dirt runway. In 1946 the city approved development of the San Jose Municipal Airport and it opened in 1949. The first commercial airline flight that landed at SJC was a DC-3 with two pilots, seven passengers and 2,550 baby chickens. Only the chickens got off at San Jose; the human passengers continued to Los Angeles. Over the years, the airport continued to expand. In 1965 tower controllers announced the airport's millionth flight and around the same time the futuristic Terminal C opened. In 2004 the airport broke ground on the first phase of the planned comprehensive replacement of all SJC terminal facilities.

The original San Jose Municipal Airport Staff posed in front of the first terminal building in 1948. *San Jose Airport Authority.*

Inaugural flight to Honolulu in 1977.
San Jose Airport Authority.

Terminal C grand opening in 1965. *San Jose Airport Authority.*

Lockheed engineers working on the Seasat, a satellite designed by Lockheed for NASA. Lockheed Martin.

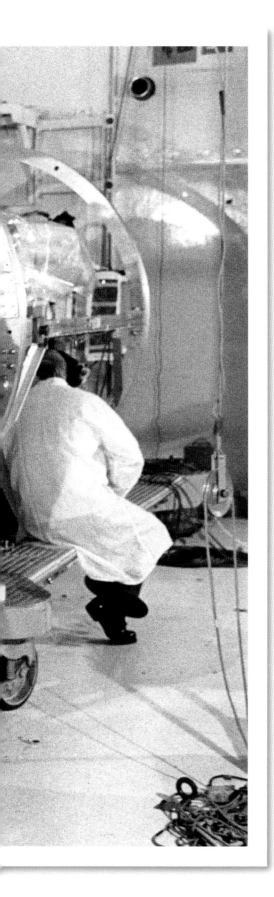

The true angel investor of Santa Clara Valley, long before the area became known as Silicon Valley, was the United States Department of Defense. As new ideas born out of Stanford University began to give way to new industries, Palo Alto became a testing ground for radio and microwave technologies and the area was soon considered a technical beacon. In the beginning, almost all of the funding for these fledgling industries came from the U.S. Government. The money flowed into the Valley from the DOD through both World Wars and finally dropped off after the end of the Cold War. It was in Palo Alto where a Stanford Graduate founded the Federal Telegraph Company. FTC is credited with the creation of the radio communication technology which allowed US Naval Ships to communicate with each other for the first time ever and just in time for World War I. In the 1930s, the residents of Santa Clara Valley pooled their money together to acquire and donate the land for what would become Moffett Field, which turned out to be a sound investment as many thousands of local jobs were created through this acquisition. Also in the 1930s and 1940s two early start-up companies born out of Stanford University, Hewlett Packard and Varian Associates, expanded rapidly thanks to their relationship with the military. During World War II, the U.S. Government and industry invested an estimated $800 million in defense plants in the Bay Area, which meant that between 1943 and 1947 about 70 new industrial plants were built in the county. Furthermore, more than $31 million was spent for defense contracts in Santa Clara county during the war years. During the Cold War and especially after the Soviets launched Sputnik in 1957, the US Government increasingly turned its attention to the potential of computers and aerospace. As weapons grew smarter and reconnaissance became the backbone of the American defense strategy, the Department of Defense focused on smart weapons, smart sensors, and stealth. At the heart of these strategies were microwaves, silicon chips, electronics and computers. And the story of the Valley continues...

EIGHT:
THE VALLEY'S
SECRET WEAPON

THE BIRTH OF THE ELECTRONIC AGE

Electrical relays circa 1910. Silicon Valley Historical Association.

As electricity caught on during the first part of the 1900s, the Bay Area (as opposed to the East Coast) was faced with the problem of carrying high tension voltage over long distances. Stanford professors and students in the newly created electrical engineering department helped solved the problem. They inaugurated a cooperative model between university and industry—the Bay Area's electrical power companies employed the Stanford high voltage laboratory and the bright minds who worked there. Together, they were able to develop the technology necessary for long distance electric power. This was the beginning of the revolutionary partnership between Stanford and private industry that would transform the area into a technological powerhouse.

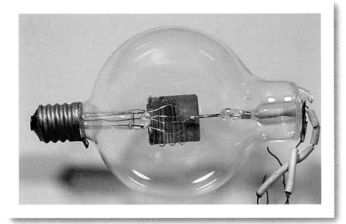

The Audion was a glass tube which was evacuated of most of its gases and contained three electrodes which, when subjected to a small electrical signal, could provide an amplifying effect. The Audion was the first vacuum tube of its kind and was critical to the development of electronic technology.

Lee de Forest with his invention, the Audion, in 1906.

In 1906 an inventor by the name of Lee de Forest invented the Audion which helped usher in the widespread use of electronics. Thus, he is considered a father of the electronic age. Vacuum tubes were critical to the development of electronic technology, which in turn drove the expansion and commercialization of radio broadcasting, television, radar, sound recording, large telephone networks as well as analog and digital computers. Also significant is the fact that Stanford University's President at the time, David Starr Jordan, invested $500 in the development of Lee DeForest's invention, which many say was the first significant venture capital investment in the region.

FEDERAL TELEGRAPH COMPANY

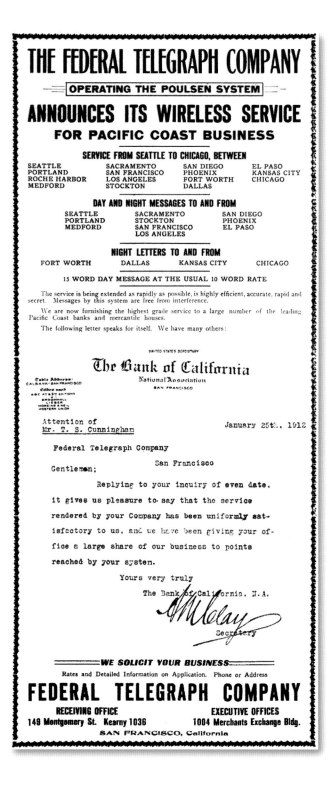

In 1909 a recent graduate from Stanford, Cyril Elwell, founded the Federal Telegraph Corporation (FTC) in Palo Alto, which created the world's first global radio communication system. Shortly after its incorporation, FTC hired Lee de Forest in order to gain use of the Audion. Stanford's president, David Starr Jordan, was the primary investor and most early employees were Stanford students. Prior to advances made at FTC, long distance transmissions would become faint over long distances. De Forest's vacuum tube enabled repeaters that restored the signal at intermediate points and dramatically improved long distance wireless communications. In 1912 FTC partnered with the Navy and was the pillar of naval communications for the US during WWI. During the war years, employment at FTC rose from 30 to 300.

FTC employees with a 500 kw arc transmitter in background. Palo Alto Historical Association.

The laboratory of Federal Telegraph Company where Lee de Forest worked:
913 Emerson in Palo Alto, which is considered the birthplace of electronics
and is now a historic landmark. Palo Alto Historical Association.

MOFFETT FIELD

Moffett Field in 1944 with 101 on the right when it was a two lane road. Moffett Field Museum.

Postcard of Moffett Field in 1944. Moffett Field Museum.

In an effort to gain the jobs and economic growth born out of government contracts, Santa Clara County citizens banded together to purchase 1,000 acres of farmland bordering the San Francisco Bay. The citizens then donated the land to the Navy to be used as the home base for the airship USS Macon. The location proved to be ideal for an airport since the area is often clear while other parts of the San Francisco Bay are covered in fog. The naval air station was authorized by an Act of Congress and signed by President Herbert Hoover in 1931. After the short-lived USS Macon, Moffett Field continued to serve as a military base. From the end of World War II until its closure, Moffett Field saw the development and use of land-based anti-submarine warfare and maritime patrol aircraft, mostly coming from a joint venture with neighbor and defense contractor, Lockheed. During the Cold War, daily anti-submarine and maritime reconnaissance missions flew out from Moffett Field to patrol along the Pacific coastline.

The Macon at Moffett Field, 1934. Moffett Field Museum.

The Macon was a rigid airship built by the Navy in 1933 to be used for reconnaissance as well as serve as a flying aircraft carrier. It was in service for less than two years. In 1935 the Macon was damaged in a storm and was lost off of California's coast. In order to accommodate such a large aircraft, Hanger One was constructed to be 1138 feet long, 308 feet wide and 198 feet high.

HENDY IRON WORKS

Hendy Iron Works machining floor, 1908. Sunnyvale Historical Society.

Hendy Iron Works was an engineering company that existed from the 1850s to the late 1940s. Originally located in San Francisco, the company relocated to Sunnyvale after being enticed with an offer of free land. The factory is perhaps best remembered for its contribution during World War II. By the end of the war, the Joshua Hendy Iron Works had supplied the engines for 28% of the Liberty ships—more than any other plant in the country. In 1947 the Joshua Hendy Iron Works was sold to the Westinghouse Corporation. In the postwar period the plant continued to produce military equipment including missile launching and control systems for nuclear powered submarines. In 1996 Westinghouse sold the plant to Northrop Grumman, which renamed it Northrop Grumman Marine Systems and continues to operate in the same plant today. The Iron Man museum now operates in a portion of the original building, which details the plant's history.

Hendy built Liberty ship for WWII. Sunnyvale Historical Society.

HENDY IRON WORKS

The crew responsible for building the Liberty ships poses for a photo to recognize their work, circa 1945. The Iron Man Museum.

President Truman visited the plant in 1943 and is shown here getting a tour of the facility. The Iron Man Museum.

FOOD MACHINERY CORPORATION

The John Bean Spray Pump, the first product of the company that would become FMC. *California Room.*

Headquarters of Anderson Barngrover in 1920 prior to its merger and name change to Food Machinery Corporation. *FMC.*

Water Buffalo produced during World War II in FMC's Santa Clara facilities. FMC.

FMC was originally founded in 1883 as the Bean Spray Pump Company in Los Gatos by John Bean. The company's first product was a pump to spray insecticide on the many fruit orchards in the area. In 1928 The Bean Spray Pump Company and Anderson Barngrover merged and after a contest was held for a new name, they decided upon Food Machinery Corporation. By the mid-1930s, FMC was the world's largest manufacturer of machinery and equipment for handling fruits, vegetables, milk, fish and meat products. With the onset of World War II, FMC entered the defense business, making amphibious tractors and tanks for the military. In 1945 the city sold 90 acres of airport land to FMC for expansion when the large employer threatened to leave the county. FMC continues to operate a number of divisions today, although the company no longer has a presence in Santa Clara Valley.

FRED TERMAN: THE FATHER OF SILICON VALLEY

Fred Terman is not given enough credit for his seminal role in creating what the Valley is today. As an engineering professor at Stanford University, he encouraged his students to start their own companies which resulted in the formation of companies like Hewlett Packard and Litton Industries. He is also part of the team credited with the idea of leasing University land to high-tech firms which paved the way for Stanford Research Park. He catapulted Stanford into the ranks of the world's first class educational institutions by chasing research grants from the Department of Defense.

Fred Terman was a Palo Alto native. His father, Lewis Terman, was a Stanford professor and is credited with popularizing the IQ test. As a teenager, Fred Terman became interested in the relatively new field of radio electronics and operated an amateur station in Palo Alto in 1917. Terman completed his undergraduate degree in chemistry and his master's degree in electrical engineering at Stanford University. He went on to earn an ScD in electrical engineering from MIT in 1924, and then returned to Stanford in 1925 to become a member of the engineering faculty. From 1925 to 1941, Terman designed a course of study and research in electronics that focused on work with vacuum tubes, circuits, and instrumentation.

During World War II, Terman directed a staff of more than 850 at the highly secret Radio Research Laboratory at Harvard University. This stealthy organization was the source of radar-blocking jammers and tunable receivers to detect radar signals used during the War. These countermeasures significantly reduced the effectiveness of enemy radar-directed weapons. After the war, Terman returned to Stanford and was appointed Dean of the School of Engineering. Under his leadership, the department received much of its funding from the Military. He served as Provost at Stanford from 1955 to 1965. During his tenure Terman greatly expanded the science, statistics and engineering departments. It was during this period that Professor Terman became concerned with the lack of economic opportunities for Stanford Engineering graduates in the Bay Area. He was part of the team that convinced the University to create the Stanford Industrial Park (now Stanford Research Park) wherein the University leased portions of its land to high-tech firms. Companies such as Varian Associates, Hewlett Packard, Eastman Kodak, General Electric, and Lockheed Corporation moved into Stanford Industrial Park. Fred Terman helped turn the Bay Area into a hotbed of innovation, and paved the way for later generations who would create Silicon Valley.

Fred Terman with his famous protégés in 1939. From left to right: Dave Packard, Bill Hewlett and Fred Terman. Stanford University Archives.

STANFORD RESEARCH PARK

Meeting in 1950 in preparation for the construction of Stanford Industrial Park. Silicon Valley Historical Association.

Stanford Industrial Park (now known as Stanford Research Park) was built in 1951 and served as the world's first cutting-edge technology-focused office park. The park covers 700 acres and is bounded by Page Mill Road and El Camino Real. Early tenants included Varian Associates, Hewlett Packard, General Electric, and Lockheed. Currently the park houses 162 buildings which are populated by 140 different companies who employ 23,000 workers.

Aerial taken in 1960 of the early Stanford Industrial Park. Sunnyvale Historical Society.

STANFORD RESEARCH PARK

Taken in 1960, this aerial is centered on Page Mill Road looking east with Junipero Serra Boulevard visible at the bottom. Palo Alto Historical Association.

PAGE MILL

EL CAMINO REAL

As a comparison, this aerial was taken in 1985 and is centered on Page Mill Road with the
Palo Alto Square office complex on the left. Palo Alto Historical Association.

PACKARD HEWLETT OR HEWLETT PACKARD?

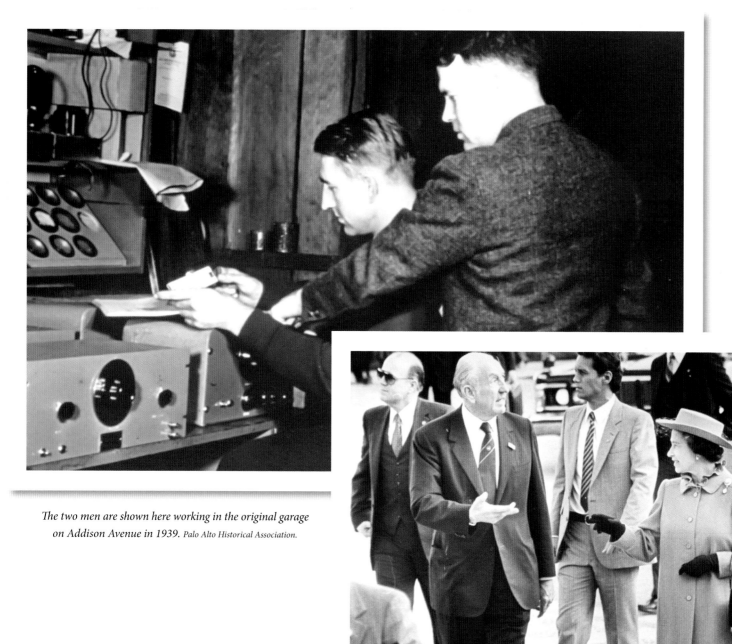

The two men are shown here working in the original garage on Addison Avenue in 1939. Palo Alto Historical Association.

David Packard and Queen Elizabeth outside HP in 1983. Palo Alto Historical Association.

David and Lucile Packard enjoying a dance together at a company party in 1945. Palo Alto Historical Association.

The two famous couples are shown here thanking their employees at a company party in 1945. Palo Alto Historical Association.

Bill Hewlett and Dave Packard became friends at Stanford in the early 1930s while obtaining degrees in electrical engineering under the mentorship of Fred Terman. After they graduated, Fred Terman convinced them to open up their own company to produce their recent invention, the audio-oscillator. Walt Disney was their very first customer who purchased their oscillators for the animation film *Fantasia*. When they first opened for business in the now famous garage, they flipped a coin to determine the name of the company—Bill won. Over the course of their 70 year friendship, there is no record of the two ever fighting. They built their company based on trust. Trust in each other and trust in their employees and customers. This philosophy is now known across the world as 'The HP Way'. Dave was considered the philosopher of the HP Way and Bill was its soul and the man who implemented it every day. This philosophy has been the basis by which many of the Bay Area start-ups based their corporate model.

A FEW OF HP's OFFICES OVER THE YEARS

367 Addison Avenue, Palo Alto where work in the now famous garage began in 1939. Palo Alto Historical Association.

395 Page Mill Drive, Palo Alto. In 1942 HP had a total of eight employees and purchased their first building. They designed it to feature an open floor plan for versatility and collaboration, which has become the model for many Silicon Valley start-ups. Palo Alto Historical Association.

690 E. Middlefield Road, Mountain View. By 1968 HP had $326 million in revenue and 15,840 employees. *City of Mountain View.*

1501 Page Mill Road, Palo Alto. In 1957 HP went public and designed their new headquarters to further implement a culture of open communication, teamwork, and innovation. They still occupy this building today. Palo Alto Historical Association.

Hewlett Packard has consistently been one of the area's largest employers and during periods of rapid expansion has occupied a wide array of facilities almost exclusively in Palo Alto and Mountain View. The company made the Fortune 500 list in 1962 with $110 million in revenue and 6250 employees. Since then, HP has continued to grow. As of 2010, the company was reporting $126 billion in revenue and 324,600 employees worldwide.

100 Mayfield Drive, Mountain View. Mayfield Mall was located at the intersection of San Antonio Road and Alma Street and served as a shopping center from 1966–1984. HP converted it into an office center in the late 1980s to accommodate their growth. City of Mountain View.

VARIAN ASSOCIATES

The Klystron. Stanford University Archives.

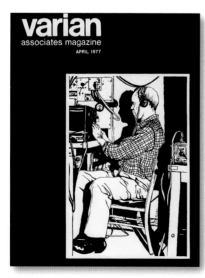

*Magazine cover for Varian with a cartoon
depicting the first amateur two-way
'moon-bounce' radio transmission.*

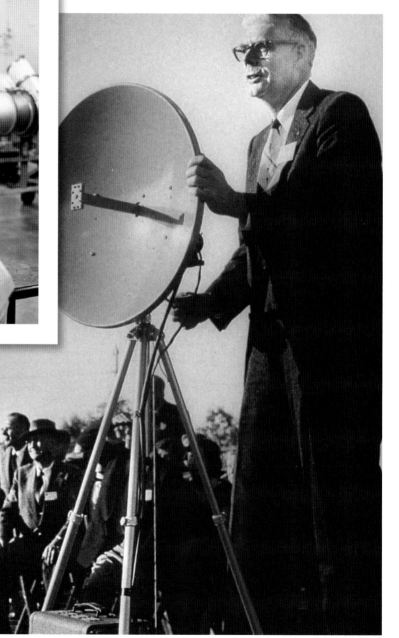

*Sigurd Varian directed a demonstration of the Klystron at the ceremony to open the
new Varian Building in The Stanford Research Park.* Palo Alto Historical Association.

Varian's initial campus, located at 3120 Hansen Way in the Stanford Research Park, is still occupied today by Varian Medical Systems. Palo Alto Historical Association.

Founded in 1948 by Stanford graduates Russell and Sigurd Varian, Edward Ginzton as well as their professor William Hansen, Varian Associates was one of the first high-tech companies in the area and maintained deep ties with Stanford. Both Fred Terman and David Packard spent time as directors. In 1953 Varian was the first tenant to occupy space in the newly formed Stanford Industrial Park. In the early years, Varian Associates subsisted almost strictly on military contracts. Their initial product was the klystron, the first tube which could generate electromagnetic waves at microwave frequencies. Their technology was instrumental in the radars used in World War II. One of Varian Associates' major contracts in the 1950s was to create a fuse for the atomic bomb. While initially supportive of military contracts, in 1958 Russell and Sigurd both expressed regret for their involvement in the development of weapons of mass destruction. The company pioneered profit-sharing, stock-ownership, insurance, and retirement plans for employees long before these benefits became mandatory. Among their early employees was bookkeeper Clara Jobs, mother of Steve Jobs. In 1999 the company was reorganized into 3 entities: Varian Medical Systems, Varian Semiconductor Equipment Associates (subsequently acquired by Applied Materials) and Varian, Inc. (subsequently acquired by Agilent Technologies).

LOCKHEED

Initially, Lockheed was located in Southern California to service the aviation industry. In 1955 they announced the creation of a missile systems division. With the goal of decentralizing their geographic locations, they purchased a 275 acre tract of land near Moffett Field in Sunnyvale. The initial construction of four buildings totaled around 250,000 square feet of office and manufacturing space. Only one year later, the new missile systems division exceeded 8,600 people in the Bay Area and so Lockheed purchased an additional 154 acres of land in Moffett Park to accommodate such rapid expansion. By 1960 the Sunnyvale population had reached 53,000—a five-fold increase over what it was just 10 years earlier. By that time, employees topped 20,000 at Lockheed Space and Missile systems. Put another way, for every family of four living in Sunnyvale 1.5 people per household worked at Lockheed. The Lockheed workforce in Sunnyvale peaked at nearly 30,000 in the mid-1980s with the fall of the Soviet Union. Lockheed is also credited with providing the talented workforce who eventually created some of the most profitable companies in Silicon Valley.

In 1960, rush hour in Sunnyvale was determined by Lockheed's massive employee base. Lockheed Martin. ▶

LOCKHEED

Aerial of Lockheed in Moffett Park in 1960. As seen here, the Lockheed campus is bordered on the east and west by orchards—on the north by the bay national refuge and on the south by the intersection of 101 and 237. Sunnyvale Historical Society.

The Polaris missile was a nuclear armed submarine-launched ballistic missile built during the Cold War by Lockheed for the United States Navy. The Polaris was first launched from Cape Canaveral in Florida in 1960. *Lockheed Martin.*

The RM-81 Agena was an American rocket upper stage and satellite support bus which was developed by Lockheed initially for the canceled U.S. Government's WS-117L reconnaissance satellite program. *Lockheed Martin.*

GTE Sylvania

1953

1963

WHISMAN ROAD

MIDDLEFIELD ROAD

The dramatic growth of the GTE Sylvania campus can be seen between the two aerials—one taken in 1953 and the other in 1963.
They eventually occupied 55 acres, which was subsequently redeveloped into housing in the mid 1990s. City of Mountain View.

Built in 1963, the "Bubble" became a local landmark located on Ferguson Drive in Mountain View. GTE Sylvania used it for the fabrication, development and testing of antennas. The 60-foot high building was totally supported by air pressure from large blowers. City of Mountain View.

Sylvania was a manufacturer of electrical equipment, including radio transceivers, vacuum tubes, semiconductors, and mainframe computers. Sylvania established a campus in 1953 in Mountain View near the intersection of Whisman and Middlefield roads. At its peak, the company owned 61 acres of land in the area and employed around 2,000 men and women. In 1958 Sylvania merged with General Telephone and Electronics and changed their name to GTE Sylvania. As with many companies in the area during the sixties and seventies, their main customer was the United States Department of Defense. Today, Sylvania is probably most well known as a manufacturer of light bulbs.

SPACE SYSTEMS LORAL

Launched in 1960, Courier was the world's first active repeater satellite. To highlight this new technology, it was used to transmit a message from President Eisenhower to the United Nations. Space Systems Loral.

Aerial of Palo Alto Campus taken in 1958. Space Systems Loral.

The company was founded as the Western Development Laboratories division of Philco Corporation in 1957 when construction began on the first building of its current campus located on Fabian Way in Palo Alto that year. The aerial above was taken in 1958 of their new headquarters located at 3825 Fabian Way, Palo Alto. After the company was acquired by Ford Motor Company in 1961 it went through a number of name changes: first to Philco-Ford; later Aeronautic Ford; later still Ford Aerospace; and finally the present name of Space Systems Loral, adopted in 1990 when it was acquired by Loral Space & Communications. It currently has around 3,000 employees in Palo Alto, a near record high. With a record of continued innovation, SS/L holds 192 active U.S. patents on satellite system technologies. Today, the company has 1.3 million square feet of office and R&D space spread over 37 buildings. The main campus sits on 77 acres.

The *Traitorous Eight* who went on to found Fairchild Semiconductor, which gave way to almost all subsequent semiconductor companies. From left: Gordon Moore, Sheldon Roberts, Eugene Kleiner, Robert Noyce, Victor Grinich, Julius Blank, Jean Hoerni and Jay Last. *City of Mountain View*

The same eight men years later in the same order as in the iconic photo initially taken in 1957. Semiconductor Industry Association.

Shockley Semiconductor opened its doors in Mountain View in 1956 and ushered in a new era for Santa Clara Valley. Shockley gathered eight of the brightest minds from across the country to work with him on his new silicon technology. These eight men were young visionaries and after leaving Shockley Semiconductor, they formed Fairchild Semiconductor which was not only outrageously successful on its own, it also cultivated almost every other semiconductor company in the Valley. In 1965 one of these eight men, Gordon Moore, predicted that the number of components in integrated circuits would continue to double every two years and his prediction has proven to be uncannily accurate. For example, in 1971 Intel created the revolutionary 4004 processor, the first commercially available microprocessor. It was the size of a fingernail and contained 2,300 transistors, which delivered the same computing power as the first electronic computer built in 1946, which filled an entire room. Fast forward to 2010 when Intel introduced their Core Processor—this chip held 560 million transistors, approximately 250,000 times more than the 1971 chip. According to the Semiconductor Industry Association, the semiconductor industry currently employs a quarter of a million people in the U.S. and supports more than one million additional American jobs. In 2011 U.S. semiconductor companies generated $153 billion in sales and are the backbone of America's trillion dollar electronics industry.

NINE: SILICON VALLEY

SHOCKLEY SEMICONDUCTOR

William Shockley was originally an employee of Bell Labs on the East Coast, a Nobel Laureate in Physics and a visiting Professor at Stanford. In 1956 he formed a company to use the element silicon for a semiconductor-based transistor instead of the then preferred element, germanium. He decided to leave the East Coast and to locate his new business on the border of Palo Alto, to be near Stanford University. Shockley pulled together a team of talented young men including Robert Noyce and Gordon Moore who have been referred to as the greatest collection of electronic geniuses ever assembled. While the impact of the technology was huge, the lifetime of the company was short. Shockley's managing style drove many employees away within a year. The company was never a big money maker and was sold to Clevite Transistor in April of 1960.

William Shockley in 1956. City of Mountain View.

The Shockley diode was one of the first semiconductor devices invented. ▶

Shockley with his mentor, Lee de Forest, whose invention, the Audion, ushered in the era of vacuum tubes that preceded the Semiconductor.
Semiconductor Industry Association.

Shockley Semiconductor headquarters located at 391 San Antonio Road, now considered a Historic Monument.

TRAITOROUS EIGHT

Celebration at Rickey's in Palo Alto. Shockley, at the head of the table, celebrated the news of his 1957 Nobel Prize in Physics with his employees shortly before their infamous departure from his company. *City of Mountain View.*

The Traitorous Eight was a term given to the eight men who left Shockley Semiconductor in 1957, due to a conflict with William Shockley. The members of the traitorous eight were between 26 and 33 years old and included Gordon Moore, Robert Noyce, Julius Blank, Victor Grinich, Jean Hoerni, Eugene Kleiner, Jay Last, and Sheldon Roberts. With the help of Arthur Rock, the group was able to get financing from Sherman Fairchild to start their own company. The newly founded Fairchild Semiconductor soon grew into a leader of the semiconductor industry and became the incubator for almost all subsequent semiconductor companies.

The Traitorous Eight, shortly after leaving Shockley in 1957. *City of Mountain View.*

FAIRCHILD SEMICONDUCTOR

The Fairchild founders from left: Gordon Moore, Sheldon Roberts, Eugene Kleiner, Robert Noyce, Victor Grinich, Julius Blank, Jean Hoerni and Jay Last. City of Mountain View.

Fairchild Semiconductor was founded in 1957 at 844 Charleston Road in Palo Alto, which is now designated California Historical Landmark #1000. Fairchild Semiconductor Corporation pioneered new products and technologies which, together with an entrepreneurial spirit and manufacturing and marketing techniques, gave birth to Silicon Valley. The "Planar Manufacturing Process" invented in 1959 revolutionized the production of semiconductor devices, which enables the manufacturing of today's transistor microprocessor and memory chips. Within a few years every other transistor company copied or licensed the Fairchild Planar Process. The company saw immense growth and grew from eight employees to over 600 in less than two years. At their peak, they employed 12,000 people, made $130 million a year and held 80% of the computer market for integrated circuits. By the late 1960s the Semiconductor Division was having serious difficulty introducing new products and satisfying fast growing customer demand—due to issues with the parent company over funds needed for new facilities, and equity to retain key employees. Ultimately, there was an exodus of much of the talent who would go on to form their own ventures including: Intel, National Semiconductor, Kleiner Perkins, Sequoia Capital, Teledyne and AMD to name a few. The company has since been through a number of management teams and ownership structures but has never regained its former profitability and prominence.

FAIRCHILD SEMICONDUCTOR

A rendering of the 64,000 square foot manufacturing plant built at 545 Whisman Road in 1958. City of Mountain View.

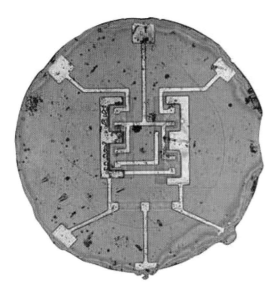

In 1960, using the planar process invented by Jean Hoerni, Fairchild engineers managed to build a circuit with four transistors on a single wafer of silicon, thereby creating the first silicon integrated circuit.

In 1968 Fairchild built their new corporate headquarters located at 464 Ellis Street in Mountain View, known as the "Rusty Bucket." It was demolished in 1993. City of Mountain View.

THE TERM SILICON VALLEY IS BORN

Don Hoefler's newsletter, Electronic News, which popularized the term Silicon Valley. Semiconductor Industry Association.

Mountain View's iconic Wagon Wheel Tavern. Stanford University Archives.

By 1970 the now iconic Silicon Valley culture was really starting to take shape. Between 1961 and 1972, at least 60 semiconductor companies were established in Silicon Valley and most were founded by former Fairchild engineers and managers. The Wagon Wheel Tavern epitomized the open culture of the area where engineers from all different companies would come to celebrate successes, recruit staff, and exchange ideas. Many credit this open, sharing culture with aiding Silicon Valley's success. Don Hoefler was a journalist famous for his newsletter Microelectronics News, the definitive tabloid of the semiconductor industry. It was he who first published the name Silicon Valley on January 10, 1971. Hoefler was often found at the Wagon Wheel gathering information for his stories.

THE FAIRCHILDREN

*Shockley Semiconductor
Founded in 1956 in Mountain
View by William Shockley.*

*Founded in 1957 when the Traitorous Eight left
Shockley to form Fairchild Semiconductor.*

*Founded in 1968 by Gordon Moore and
Robert Noyce after they left Fairchild.*

*In 1967 National Semiconductor relocated to
Santa Clara from the East Coast after hiring away
five executives from Fairchild Semiconductor.*

*Founded in 1969 by a group of former
executives from Fairchild Semiconductor.*

*Founded 1974 by Federico
Faggin, who helped invent the
8080 microprocessor at Intel.*

*Founded in 1981 by Wilfred Corrigan,
former CEO of Fairchild Semiconductor.*

Intel employees at their new building in Santa Clara at the corner of Bowers Avenue and Central Expressway in 1971. Intel Corporation.

In 1968 Gordan Moore and Robert Noyce left Fairchild Semiconductor to found Intel using $2.5 million raised by Arthur Rock. Their company name is a combination of the words integrated and electronics. Andy Grove, who would go on to be the CEO of Intel, was their first hire. By 1971 the company had gone public raising $6.8 million and moved into a newly constructed headquarters sitting on 26 acres in Santa Clara on the corner of Central Expressway and Bowers Avenue. In 1974 Intel announced the 8080 microprocessor, perhaps the single most important product of the 20th century. At the time, it was the most complicated mass produced item ever built—each one with as many architectural features as a medium sized city and the product of programs as complicated as the Manhattan Project. It featured 4,500 transistors making it ten times faster than its predecessors. In 1978 after only ten years in business, Intel was up to 10,000 employees and by 1983 had reached $1 billion in revenue. They remain one of the leading chip companies in the world.

Robert Noyce breaking ground for the new facility in 1970. Intel Corporation.

THE MEN BEHIND INTEL

ROBERT NOYCE is perhaps most famous for co-inventing the integrated circuit. Robert was an east coast native and liked handicraft from early on. While in college, Noyce attended a physics course where he was introduced to the first transistors from Bell Labs and was hooked. After college, he attended MIT to get his PhD and upon graduation went to work for Philco Ford. Two years later, he was contacted by William Shockley and moved west to join the team. After founding Fairchild Semiconductor, his first years there were the most intellectually fertile time for Noyce. Seven of his 17 patents, including his most important, the integrated circuit, date from the 18 months after the company was launched. In 1979 Noyce received the national medal of Science from president Jimmy Carter.

GORDON MOORE is most famous for his predictive observations of microchip evolution, referred to as Moore's Law. He was born in Pescadero, a small beach-side community between Santa Cruz and Half Moon Bay in California. He graduated from Caltech then worked for Lawrence Livermore Labs before being recruited by William Shockley. Moore was one of the founders of Fairchild Semiconductor and worked there for 11 years before leaving to found Intel with Robert Noyce. In 1965 while serving as Fairchild's R&D director, he wrote an article for Electronics Magazine on the future of the semiconductor industry. He observed that over the history of computing hardware the number of transistors on integrated circuits doubled approximately every two years. This trend has continued for more than half a century and has been a driving force of technological and social change.

ANDY GROVE is best known for transforming Intel from a manufacturer of memory chips into one of the world's dominant producers of microprocessors. During his tenure as CEO, Grove oversaw a 4,500% increase in Intel's market capitalization from $4 billion to $197 billion, making it the world's 7th largest company, with 64,000 employees. Grove was Gordon Moore and Robert Noyce's first hire. He served as Intel's president starting in 1979, its CEO in 1987, and its Chairman and CEO in 1997. He relinquished his CEO title in May 1998, having been diagnosed with prostate cancer although remained chairman of the board until November 2004. Under his leadership, most of the company's revenues were reinvested in research and development, along with building new facilities, in order to produce improved and faster microprocessors.

Robert Noyce and Gordon Moore in 1984. Intel Corporation.

From left to Right: Andy Grove, Robert Noyce and Gordon Moore. Intel Corporation.

NATIONAL SEMICONDUCTOR

Intel founder Robert Noyce, and the CEO of National Semiconductor, Charlie Sporck, playing chess. Many attribute the success of the Valley on the information sharing and problem solving that takes place even between competing companies. Texas Instruments.

Charlie Sporck, CEO of National Semiconductor from 1967 to 1991, was also known for his love of cigars. *Texas Instruments.*

National Semiconductor was founded in Connecticut in 1959. In 1967 it shifted its headquarters to Santa Clara in California to attract the talent employed in the area at Fairchild and HP. One of the Fairchilders they recruited was Charles Sporck, the operations manager at Fairchild directly under Bob Noyce. Charles Sporck was appointed President and CEO of National. Sporck steered the company towards the growing market for commercial and industrial applications, thereby lessening their dependence on the highly competitive military and aerospace market. Additionally, Sporck's cost control efforts led him to be one of the pioneers in the semiconductor industry to outsource final manufacturing of integrated circuits, especially to Southeast Asia. Under his management, National Semiconductor became the first semiconductor company to reach $1 billion annual sales in 1981. Texas Instruments acquired National Semiconductor in 2011.

National Semiconductor

National Semiconductor CORPORATION

FIRST ANNUAL REPORT

DECEMBER 31, 1959

ADVANCED MICRO DEVICES

Jerry Sanders formed AMD in 1969 and served as chairman and CEO until 2002. In 1961 Jerry moved West from his home in Chicago when he was recruited to Fairchild Semiconductor. He quickly rose to a succession of management positions and seemed headed for the top. But new management came in at Fairchild and Sanders' style made them uneasy. They fired him. Sanders got together with other ex-Fairchilders to start AMD. Sanders wrote the business plan and developed a program to go out and raise money. Sanders jokes that while Bob Noyce often told the story that it took him five minutes to raise five million dollars it was the other way around for Sanders—taking him five million minutes to raise five dollars. But Sanders was determined—he raised $1.5 million and in 1969 AMD was born. Sanders is regarded as one of the most colorful, clever and bold in the generation that founded the semiconductor industry and Silicon Valley. Jerry was an engaging leader with the motto, "Put people first, products and profits will follow." AMD was the first company to give every employee shares of its stock and the first company to participate in profit sharing. He had a taste for outlandish and theatrical spirit-rousing such as: materializing from a cloud of smoke at a sales meeting wearing a pink jumpsuit; or staring down from in-house movie posters as "Illinois Jerry," a character fighting the evil forces against AMD.

Jerry Sanders in 1980. AMD.

The AMD management team at the ground breaking ceremony for their new Sunnyvale headquarters on Thompson Way in Sunnyvale in 1969. AMD.

The completed 901 Thompson building at the right along with the later two story expansion at 902 Thompson, circa 1970. AMD

LSI Logic

LSI founders from left to right: Mick Bohn, Wilf Corrigan, Rob Walker, and Bill O'Meara.

LSI Logic was founded in Milpitas in 1981 by Wilf Corrigan as a semiconductor company after he left his post as CEO of Fairchild Semiconductor in 1979. The other three founders were Bill O'Meara, Rob Walker and Mick Bohn. Corrigan was CEO for LSI for over 20 years until 2005. The initial $6 million round of funding was led by ex-Fairchilder Don Valentine who by that point had started Sequoia Capital. The firm went public in 1983—netting $153 million, the largest tech IPO up to that point. LSI developed the industry's first line of ASIC (application-specific integrated circuits) which let customers create custom chips by use of leading-edge proprietary CAD tools. Renamed LSI Corporation, the company today focuses on chips that handle the massive amounts of data generated by our digital society.

APPLIED MATERIALS

The first office of Applied Materials in 1967—a 750 square foot industrial unit in Mountain View. *Applied Materials.*

Applied Materials founder, Michael McNeilly. *Applied Materials.*

A rendering of the new Applied Materials campus on Bowers Avenue in 1974. *Applied Materials.*

*Michael McNeilly & Walter Benzing pioneered epitaxial
deposition equipment at Applied Materials.* SEMI.

*In 1972 the AMS 2000/2001 Continuous Silo Reactor system changed
the concept of equipment architecture from "batch-at-a-time" to
high throughput continuous processing.* Applied Materials.

Applied Materials, originally known as Applied Materials Technology, was founded in 1967 by Michael McNeilly at the ripe old age of 28 with a $7,500 loan from his father-in-law in a 750 square foot industrial unit in Mountain View. The initial goal of Applied Materials was to supply the rapidly growing semiconductor companies with the materials and equipment needed for their manufacturing processes. While most of the large semiconductor companies had their own internal process development capabilities, the semiconductor industry was spawning many new device start-ups who needed equipment for their ventures. McNeilly credits the early success of the company to the relationship he had with the management team of Fairchild through informal meetings at the Wagon Wheel and playing basketball for the Fairchild team. The early board of directors and investors in Applied Materials included Bob Noyce, Tom Perkins, Jean Hoerni and Charlie Sporck—all early members of Fairchild Semiconductor. Once Applied raised the capital they needed to grow the business, they moved into an 18,000 square foot building on San Ysidro Way in Santa Clara, directly across the street from National Semiconductor, and grew the business to 100 employees and revenues of about $10 million in their first year there. McNeilly instituted a policy early on that any prototype system built for a customer must also be installed in a lab in the Applied Materials space, which was the first cleanroom demo lab in the industry. In 1972 Applied Materials dropped 'Technology' from their name and went public. In 1974 they relocated from San Ysidro to a larger building on Bowers Avenue. Today, Applied materials has nearly $9 billion in annual sales and holds over 10,000 patents.

By the 1950s Santa Clara Valley was already becoming defined by its culture of entrepreneurship. However, in the 1950s and into the early 1960s, there was no such thing as venture capital, which meant a young entrepreneur who wanted to start a company essentially had two options for financing. The first option was to secure a decent sized military contract, which paid for both the upfront R&D costs and the purchase of the final product. Hewlett Packard and Varian followed this approach: they secured military contracts and depended on them for their survival. The second option was to woo an established company to sponsor the new venture. Shockley Semiconductor and Fairchild Semiconductor were funded in this manner as each was initially backed by established corporations (Beckman Instruments and Fairchild Camera, respectively). However, in the late 1950s things started to change as local companies began to go public: Varian in 1956, Hewlett Packard in 1957, and Ampex in 1958. To potential investors, this offered a means of liquidity. Also in 1958, the SBIC Act was passed which provided 4:1 leverage for any investment institution that provided funds to small innovative companies. This meant that for every $1 private investors lent to a small business, the U.S. Government would invest an additional $4. A large concentration of SBIC investment groups set up in the Bay Area to tap into the emerging microwave and semiconductor start-up companies. The exponential growth of the technology sector in Santa Clara Valley helped propel Sandhill Road in Menlo Park into the premier venture capital region of the world. This chapter explores some of the pioneers.

Ten:
Venture Capital
& Sand Hill Road

SAND HILL ROAD

Sand Hill Road in 1904, facing west. Ford Land Company.

Sand Hill Road in 1970, taken from the air over highway 280 and focused on the newly constructed 3000 Sand Hill Circle development in Menlo Park. Ford Land Company.

VENTURE FUNDING BY REGION, 1995 - 2012

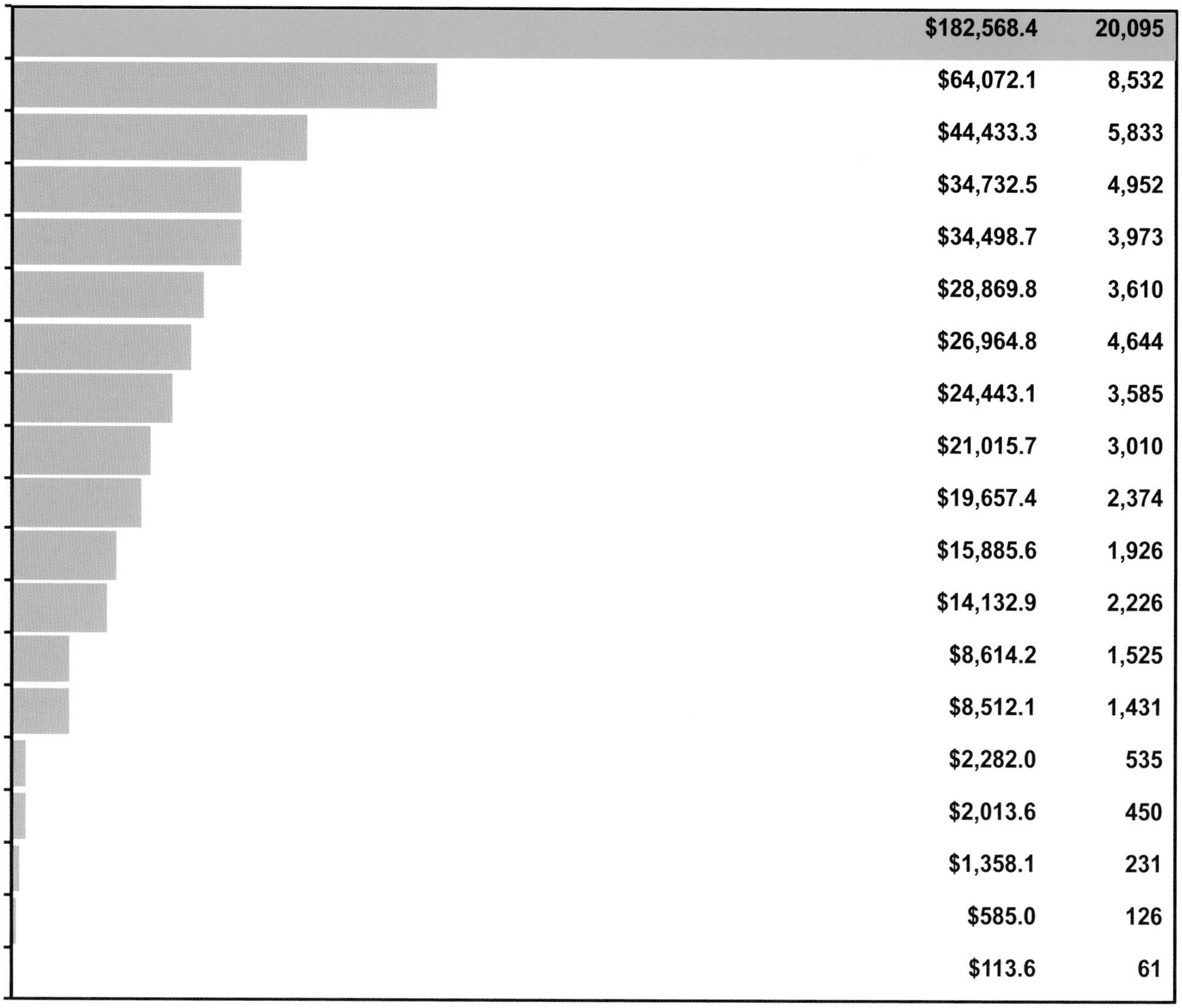

Region		Funding ($M)	Deals
Silicon Valley		$182,568.4	20,095
New England		$64,072.1	8,532
NY Metro		$44,433.3	5,833
Southeast		$34,732.5	4,952
LA/Orange County		$34,498.7	3,973
Texas		$28,869.8	3,610
Midwest		$26,964.8	4,644
DC/Metroplex		$24,443.1	3,585
Northwest		$21,015.7	3,010
San Diego		$19,657.4	2,374
Colorado		$15,885.6	1,926
Philadelphia Metro		$14,132.9	2,226
North Central		$8,614.2	1,525
SouthWest		$8,512.1	1,431
South Central		$2,282.0	535
Upstate NY		$2,013.6	450
Sacramento/N.Cal		$1,358.1	231
AK/HI/PR		$585.0	126
Unknown		$113.6	61
Total US		**$534,753.0**	**69,119**

The chart above reflects data complied by Price Waterhouse Coopers on the venture capital industry dating back to 1995. Silicon Valley has seen over $182 billion in investments placed into approximately 20,000 start-up companies over the last seventeen years. That is more than the next four regions combined.

Sand Hill Road in 1920. Silicon Valley Historical Association.

ARTHUR ROCK

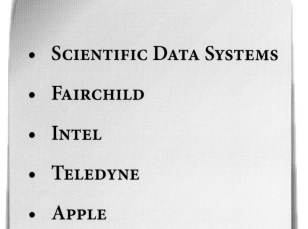

- **SCIENTIFIC DATA SYSTEMS**
- **FAIRCHILD**
- **INTEL**
- **TELEDYNE**
- **APPLE**

Arthur Rock was born in 1926 in New York and attended Syracuse University for his undergraduate degree and later Harvard Business School. Upon graduation from Harvard, Rock joined the Wall Street investment firm, Hayden, Stone & Co. In 1956 when the "Traitorous Eight" were looking to leave Shockley Semiconductor, it turned out that one of them, Gene Kleiner, had a father with an account at Hayden, Stone & Co. Gene wrote a letter to his father's investment house saying, "A lot of us like working together. Do you think there's a company that would hire the whole group?" It was Arthur Rock who was instrumental in getting "The Eight" not to join another company but to start their own. He approached all of the wealthy clients he had in the attempt to raise funding for their new venture, but almost everyone said no. When close to giving up, he found an investor: Sherman Fairchild, who decided to invest $1.5 million in the new start-up as a way to diversify the product line for Fairchild Camera. After the wild success of Fairchild Semiconductor, Arthur Rock decided to chase the wave and moved to California in 1961. He teamed up with Thomas Davis Jr. and founded California's first true venture capital firm: Davis & Rock. The investment company operated until 1968 and during those seven years they funded 15 new companies. The firm hit it really big with an investment in Scientific Data Systems, or SDS — one of the first companies to use microchips in computers. Davis and Rock invested close to $260,000 and in only eight years Xerox purchased SDS for almost $1 billion. In 1968 when Robert Noyce and Gordon Moore split from Fairchild to form Intel, Rock raised the $2.5 million needed to fund the creation of Intel. In fact, he invested $300,000 of his own money and acted as the first president of the company. Another major milestone for Rock was meeting Steve Jobs and Steve Wozniak and his subsequent investment in Apple in 1978. At the time, he bought 640,000 shares of Apple at nine cents per share for a total investment of $57,000. Three years later Apple went public and Rock's $57,000 became $14 million.

TOMMY DAVIS AND THE MAYFIELD FUND

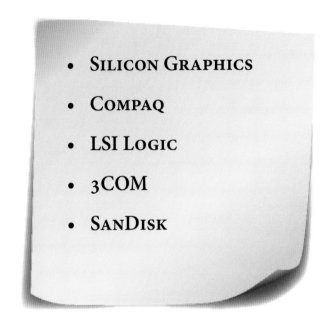

- **SILICON GRAPHICS**
- **COMPAQ**
- **LSI LOGIC**
- **3COM**
- **SANDISK**

Tommy Davis Jr. was born in 1912 in Cincinnati and earned his Bachelor of Arts and Law degrees from Harvard University. After serving in World War II, he began working for the Kern County Land Company in California's Central Valley. With the technology boom that was beginning to take hold in Santa Clara Valley, he decided to get out of land development and use his own money to make angel investments in fledgling technology companies. In 1963 he teamed up with Arthur Rock and after some wildly successful investments together, they decided to go their separate ways. In 1969 Tommy Davis teamed up with Wally Davis (no relation) and with an investment from Stanford University, they founded the Mayfield Fund. The first fund was around $3 million. Since then Mayfield has raised over $2.8 billion of investor commitments across 13 private equity funds. They have invested in more than 530 companies resulting in over 100 Initial Public Offerings and more than 100 mergers and acquisitions. The firm is still headquartered on Sand Hill Road in Menlo Park.

THE DRAPER DYNASTY

William Draper Jr. in 1978.

Draper Fisher Jurvetson.

From left to right: Bill Draper III, Tim Draper and William Draper Jr. Taken in 1978.

Draper Fisher Jurvetson.

William Draper III in 1959.

Draper Fisher Jurvetson.

Steve Jurvetson, Tim Draper and John Fisher in 1985 upon the founding of Draper Fisher Jurvetson. Draper Fisher Jurvetson.

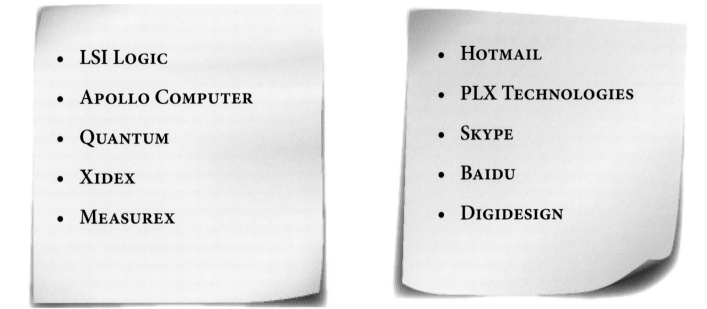

- LSI LOGIC
- APOLLO COMPUTER
- QUANTUM
- XIDEX
- MEASUREX

- HOTMAIL
- PLX TECHNOLOGIES
- SKYPE
- BAIDU
- DIGIDESIGN

The Draper family dynasty began with William Draper Jr. in the late 1950s. William Draper Jr. grew up on the East Coast and had a background in investment banking. In 1958 Draper got together with Rowan Gaither, the founder of the Rand Corporation, and Frederick L. Anderson, a retired Air Force general. Together they formed what was the first venture capital firm to be structured as a limited partnership. Draper, Gaither & Anderson remained in existence through 1966.

William's son, Bill Draper III, followed in his father's footsteps. He graduated from Yale University in 1950, a year after George H. W. Bush. Bill Draper went on to attend Harvard Business School and studied under professor Georges Doriot, who is credited with mentoring many of the early venture capitalists. In 1959 Bill Draper came to work as an associate at his father's newly formed firm. He canvased the area, approaching any storefront with the word technology in its name to ask if they wanted some capital in exchange for equity. A few years later in 1962, Bill left his fathers firm to co-found the venture capital firm Draper & Johnson Investment Company with his good friend Pitch Johnson. In 1965 Draper founded Sutter Hill Ventures, which fifty years later, remains one of the top venture capital firms in the country. During his twenty years as the senior partner of Sutter Hill, Draper helped to organize and finance several hundred high technology manufacturing companies including Apollo Computer, Dionex, Integrated Genetics, Quantum, Xidex, Measurex, Hybritech, and LSI Logic. In 2005 he received the Vision Award from SD Forum and was inducted into the Dow Jones Venture Capital Hall of Fame. In 2006 he received the Silicon Valley Fast 50 Lifetime Achievement Award.

Bill's son, Tim, continued in the family legacy and in 1985 started his own venture capital firm, Draper Fisher Jurvetson. He has a BS in Electrical Engineering from Stanford University and an MBA from Harvard Business School. He has been named #52 of the 100 most influential Harvard alumni, and #7 on the Forbes Midas List. He was named the #1 venture capital deal maker in 2008 by Always-On. His investments include Skype, Baidu, Parametric Technology, Hotmail, PLX Technologies, Digidesign and hundreds of others.

GENE KLEINER & TOM PERKINS

From left to right: Brook Byers, Frank Caufield, Tom Perkins, and Eugene Kleiner. KPCB.

- **TANDEM COMPUTERS**
- **GENENTECH**
- **APPLIED MATERIALS**

In 1972 Gene Kleiner, an original founder of Fairchild Semiconductor and Thomas Perkins, a leader of Hewlett Packard's early computer hardware division, formed their own venture capital firm using $8 million from a private investor. In the beginning many of their deals lost money and after a couple of years it was apparent they needed to do something different. That something happened to come in the form of an opportunity to invest in Tandem Computers under the leadership of larger-than-life Texan, Jimmy Treybig. It was an interesting time in the computer market in 1974: IBM controlled the mainframe market and there was little room for competitors. But Tom Perkins saw a need in the market for stable mainframe computers that would never fail, regardless of the environment. His intuition paid off. The development of Tandem's no fail mainframe led to its exponential growth. Tandem made the Fortune 500 list by 1982. Perkins' original investment of $1.4 million in 1974 turned Tandem into a $3 billion company by the time it sold to Compaq in 1997.

DON VALENTINE & SEQUOIA CAPITAL

- **APPLE COMPUTER**
- **ATARI**
- **LSI LOGIC**
- **CISCO SYSTEMS**

Don Valentine grew up in a suburb of New York City and got his start in technology working in vacuum tube sales for Sylvania. In 1959 Valentine realized the future of the technology market was in semiconductors, and that meant California. He left the East Coast to begin work for Fairchild Semiconductor. He worked his way through the ranks of the sales team, where he is credited with hiring many of the bright young men who went on to become industry leaders—including Jerry Sanders (founder of AMD), Jack Gifford (founder and CEO of Maxim) and Mike Markkula (initial investor and CEO of Apple). In 1968 Don Valentine joined Charles Sporck as a defector from Fairchild to help found National Semiconductor. In 1972 he left the semiconductor business and founded Sequoia Capital with an $8 million investment. One of his first investments was in Atari in 1974. A few years later, it was Valentine who put Steve Jobs and Steve Wozniak in touch with their initial investor and CEO, Mike Markkula. Since then he and his Sequoia Capital Partners have participated in the financing of over 500 technology companies. Some of the more famous investments include: Atari in 1974; LSI Logic in 1981; Electronic Arts, which was started in Sequoia's office in 1982; and Cisco Systems in 1987.

Before the 1960s most office and manufacturing buildings in Santa Clara Valley were constructed by the companies themselves as the need arose. The concept of speculative development, i.e. constructing buildings without a specific occupant in mind, only became a viable business model around the same time that venture capital did. With the introduction of the semiconductor and the emergence of the start-up culture in the Valley, a need arose for an already existing supply of commercial space where young companies could grow quickly and relatively inexpensively. Following the boom and bust cycles of the technology companies for which the real estate has been constructed, the commercial market in Silicon Valley has seen periods of rapid growth followed by periods of oversupply and insufficient demand. This chapter explores some of the early pioneers.

ELEVEN: COMMERCIAL REAL ESTATE DEVELOPMENT

PALO ALTO - 1950

EL CAMINO REAL

PAGE MILL

FOOTHILL EXPRESSWAY

ARASTRADERO

SILICON VALLEY: *The History in Pictures*

PALO ALTO - 1982

EL CAMINO REAL

PAGE MILL

FOOTHILL EXPRESSWAY

ARASTRADERO

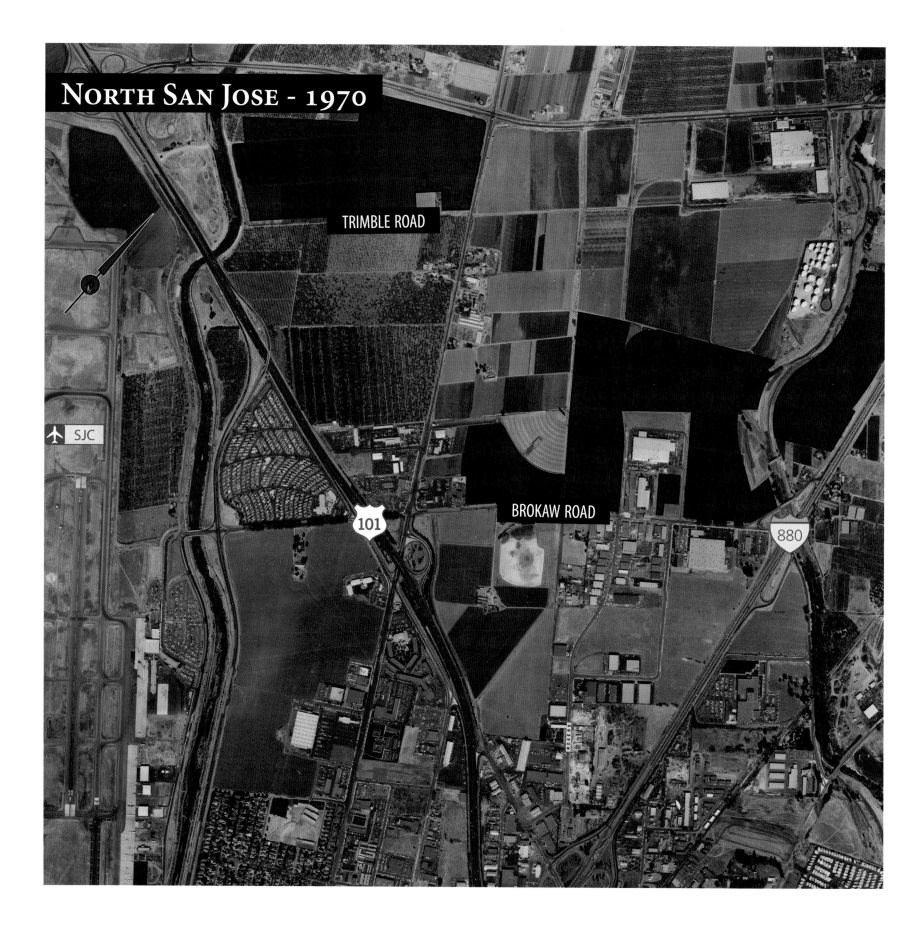

NORTH SAN JOSE - 1970

TRIMBLE ROAD

BROKAW ROAD

SJC

101

880

ROGERS

NORTH SAN JOSE - 1983

TRIMBLE ROAD

SJC

101

BROKAW ROAD

880

SUNNYVALE COMMERCIAL TENANTS IN 1969

Forty years ago Sunnyvale was mostly farmland with the occasional commercial building here and there. As one would expect, the companies who occupied such buildings reflected the economy of the time: mostly defense and early semiconductor related companies. To help put things in perspective, consider that in 1960 the population of Santa Clara County was one third the size it is today. The 1960s saw an inflection point when the population of Santa Clara County surpassed its once larger neighbor, San Francisco County. In 1960 both counties had a population of around 700,000. Today, San Francisco County has 825,000 residents whereas Santa Clara County has 1.8 million.

1. LOCKHEED

2. FAIRCHILD SEMICONDUCTOR®

3. National Semiconductor

4. Westinghouse

5. memorex™

6. signetics

7. AMPEX

101

ARQUES AVENUE

LAWRENCE EXPY

CENTRAL EXPY

KIFER ROAD

PEERY-ARRILLAGA

In the early 1970s on the recommendation of a bank executive, John Arrillaga and Richard Peery formed a partnership with a $2,000 investment. For nearly four decades, the company's signature buildings with red-tiled roofs, smoked-glass windows and rock-encrusted walls transformed acres of orchards into the entrepreneurial tech haven of Silicon Valley. Peery & Arrillaga foresaw the needs of the rapidly growing technology companies. Their generic buildings were ready for occupancy before a company knew it would need it. Their early construction used the cost effective method of concrete tilt-up, where concrete was poured into molds on the ground and then "tilted up'" into place. They built their empire with their own capital by building one building at a time, freeing them from having to rely on bank loans. As with Bill Hewlett and Dave Packard, these real estate barons built relationships based on trust. Their sense of fairness and honesty permeated their dealings with tenants, vendors and competitors. When inducted into a commercial real estate hall of fame, Peery asked Arrillaga, "How many partnerships last so long?" Arrillaga replied, "We're more like brothers than we are partners. Thank you for the friendship."

PEERY-ARRILLAGA

*First Generation: 1970–1980. Concrete tilt-up buildings with minimal window line. Office
up front with the balance of the building dedicated to lab, manufacturing and distribution
so as to meet the needs of early semiconductor companies. Peery-Arrillaga.*

*Second Generation: 1980–1990. Buildings constructed with three sides of glass in single or two story configurations.
Business Parks built for multiple tenants came into fashion around this time as well as landscaping featuring
ponds and fountains. Demountable interior walls were often used to re-purpose the space. Peery-Arrillaga.*

Third Generation: 1990–2000. Typically two to three stories, these buildings were characterized by an expanded window line with more emphasis on office space but maintaining a lab and warehouse component. Peery-Arrillaga.

Fourth Generation: 2000 to present. Steel frame construction with four sides of glass and smaller floor plates so natural light floods the entire space to accommodate the changing workforce. As opposed to the original "tech workers" of the 1960s who worked primarily on the manufacturing floor, today most tech workers hold desk jobs. Peery-Arrillaga.

JOHN A. SOBRATO

A postcard from John's Rendezvous circa 1940, which was owned and operated by John Sobrato's father. Sobrato Development.

John A. Sobrato was born in San Francisco, the only child of Ann and John M. Sobrato. His father emigrated from Italy after working as a chef for the American army during World War I and eventually opened his own restaurant, John's Rendezvous in North Beach. WWII-era food shortages prompted the Sobrato family to purchase five acres in Atherton to raise poultry and produce to support the restaurant. Sobrato was only twelve when his father died. With a young son to support, his mother, Ann Sobrato took English classes, sold the restaurant and reinvested the proceeds in additional properties on the peninsula, discovering her penchant for real estate.

MIDTOWN REALTY

BUYING?   SELLING?

In either case, our competent staff is at your service. Our selection of properties is one of the largest on the Peninsula. Whether you are looking for fast action in the sale of your home, or if you are looking for a TRUE VALUE and a SOUND INVESTMENT, it will pay you to check with us.

Ann Sobrato with her billboard for one of the area's first speculative developments. *Sobrato Development.*

CARL E. BERG   JOHN A. SOBRATO

Newspaper advertisement for Midtown Realty picturing Carl Berg and John Sobrato, from the early 1960s. Sobrato Development.

While at Santa Clara University, John got started selling Eichler homes in Palo Alto and ended up becoming the top salesman almost overnight. At the age of 21, he took over the management of the company and renamed it Midtown Realty. In 1961 John Sobrato, along with the assistance of his mom Ann, developed his first commercial building for Lockheed Corporation, a 14,000 square foot concrete tilt-up located at 1260 Birchwood Avenue in Sunnyvale.

Sobrato's first commercial development—a build to suit building for Lockheed. Sobrato Development.

JOHN A. SOBRATO

Construction of the 200,000 square foot Ahmdal campus in Sunnyvale in the early 1970s. Sobrato Development.

In 1962 Sobrato convinced his friend and mortgage broker, Carl Berg, to join Midtown Realty as a partner. In 1969 John Sobrato and Carl Berg transitioned out of home sales and into commercial development. Their first project was a building on the corner of Lawrence and Central Expressways on a three acre property acquired for $1.10 per square foot from the city of Sunnyvale. A few years later they constructed a 200,000 square foot campus for Ahmdal at 1250 East Arques Avenue, which was just down the street from their initial development. This was the first major campus in the area built by developers instead of the company itself, which gave Sobrato and Berg credibility as one of the first commercial real estate developers.

1991: 1 Infinite Loop, Cupertino. Sobrato Development.

2000: 4980 Great America Parkway, Santa Clara. Sobrato Development.

2001: 2811-2821 Mission College, Santa Clara. Sobrato Development.

2002: 2701-2731 San Tomas Expressway, Santa Clara. Sobrato Development.

In 1974 Sobrato sold Midtown Realty to concentrate on the commercial development of properties in the rapidly emerging high technology industry. After nine years and 2.3 million square feet of development, Sobrato and Berg split to form separate companies and the Sobrato Development Company was founded. Sobrato is probably best known and most proud of his 875,000 square foot campus development for Apple Computer completed in 1991. Today his company controls 7.5 million square feet across 75 buildings and 400 acres of land. Many famous technology companies have called one of his developments "home" including Apple Computer, Netflix, NVIDIA and Citrix.

DAVE BROWN AND ORCHARD COMMERCIAL

*Dave Brown, Freshmen Class President at Claremont
Men's College in 1958.* Orchard Properties.

Dave Brown was born in Coronado, California in 1939, the oldest of five children. He attended Claremont Men's College in the greater Los Angeles area for his undergraduate degree and then attended the Wharton School of Business. After receiving his MBA, Dave Brown worked for a number of real estate developers in the Bay Area. In 1969 he was given a job by the Boise Cascade Building Company to develop a number of industrial business parks in Northern California from scratch. With the capital provided by Boise Cascade, he acquired a number of parcels of land. The largest by far was around 1,400 acres in North San Jose. The land area in San Jose that he acquired is part of what's called the Golden Triangle: it is bordered by Highway 880 to the East and Highway 101 to the West. In 1971 Boise Cascade decided they were no longer interested in being in the real estate business and instructed Dave Brown to put up for sale all of the properties he had recently acquired. He brought the properties to the market and tried to sell them for over two years. As time went on, it became apparent that no one was interested in the land because it was still so rural. At the time, the main road through North San Jose was North First Street, which was a two-lane road flanked by irrigation ditches and surrounded by orchards.

Boise Cascade Industrial Park advertisement from the early 1970s. Orchard Properties.

DAVE BROWN AND ORCHARD COMMERCIAL

Orchard Commercial's first real estate transaction was the sale of land for $1 per square foot to Sun Electric. Orchard Properties.

Left with no other option, Boise Cascade sold Dave Brown their Northern California real estate holdings at a 50% discount. In May of 1973, Dave Brown launched Orchard Properties to manage the land he had acquired. The name of the newly formed real estate company was fitting, as most of the land he acquired was covered in orchards. From the inception of Orchard Properties in 1973 through 1976, the real estate market hit a period of oversupply and the future of Orchard Commercial was very tenuous. It took 18 months to make their first real estate deal: a sale of land for $1 per square foot to Sun Electric. Then the market took off. From 1977 through 1983 Orchard was developing over one million square feet a year. As tech proliferated, they went on to develop seven million square feet, primarily in North San Jose.

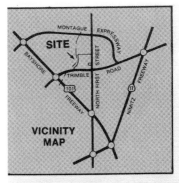

Located between Highways 101 and 17 in North San Jose, the Orchard Technology Park offers excellent ingress and egress and is situated near the eastern foothills where the bulk of new housing is being constructed.

ORCHARD TECHNOLOGY PARK

Advertisement for the Orchard Technology Park, circa 1980. Orchard Properties.

CARL BERG AND MISSION WEST PROPERTIES

A postcard from Tucumcara, New Mexico where
Carl Berg grew up. *Mission West.*

One of Carl Berg's early sales jobs was selling
Dr. Pepper while in high school. *Mission West.*

Carl Berg grew up in Tucumcara, New Mexico on Route 66 and was a natural salesman from an early age. He attended the University of New Mexico with dreams of becoming an investment banker on Wall Street. With this aim, he got a job at the nicest motel in Albuquerque so he might build rapport with the businessmen who stayed there. While a junior in college, he met a successful home builder who offered him a job in his mortgage brokerage division. After graduation Carl moved to Fort Worth to run the entire mortgage division where he was extremely successful in restoring the division to profitability, mainly by streamlining the process of responding to customer letters and concerns. A couple of years into his stint in Fort Worth, the economy had a downturn and Carl left for another job opportunity in El Paso.

One of Carl Berg's first commercial developments. Developed in conjunction with John Sobrato, it was a campus built for Four Phase Systems on the land where Apple's Infinity Loop campus currently stands. Mission West.

John Sobrato helping Carl Berg prepare for his wedding. Mission West.

In 1960 Carl moved to California to work for another mortgage brokerage company where he stayed for a couple of years before leaving to work with John Sobrato at Midtown Realty selling Eichler homes in Palo Alto. Sobrato and Berg's first commercial development was a 30,000 square foot building in Sunnyvale on the corner of Lawrence and Central Expressways. But the project that put them on the map was the campus they built in 1979 on 50 acres at the corner of De Anza Boulevard and Highway 9, bought from the Mariani family for $50,000 an acre. Here the two developers built 800,000 square feet for Four-Phase Systems in six months. In order to meet such a tight timeline they employed four different contractors, one for each building.

CARL BERG AND MISSION WEST PROPERTIES

Caricature of real estate baron, Carl Berg. *Mission West.*

Carl Berg with a road side advertisement for a build to suit real estate development. *Mission West.*

Early on, Berg also began investing in the companies who were coming to him for office space. In 1978 John Sobrato and Carl Berg decided to divide their assets so that Sobrato could focus strictly on commercial real estate development and Carl could pursue his passion for both real estate and venture funding. Shortly after his split from Sobrato, Berg gathered 16 Silicon Valley engineers to advise him on future investments, which was the most lucrative period of his investment career. Of the 38 investments they made during this time, all but one were successful. He credits the successes to the fact that he required a 100% understanding of the company and its competitive landscape before he invested. Two of the investments alone, Sun Microsystems and IDT, made him a fortune.

The building Carl Berg built for Microsoft in Mountain View off 101. Mission West.

A five building build to suit development in South San Jose developed by Carl Berg for Ciena. Prior to the sale of most of the real estate holdings to Divco West, Mission West was by far the largest commercial real estate holder in South San Jose. Mission West.

After Berg split with John Sobrato, he managed his real estate holdings with his brother Clyde and created Berg & Berg Properties. Berg applied his business acumen to his real estate holdings. In 1998 Carl created Mission West Properties as a REIT which allowed him to raise additional capital to continue to grow the business. Amazingly, Berg never had more than eight people on staff running a public company with over a billion dollars in assets. In late 2012 Carl Berg wound down the Mission West REIT and sold the majority of his real estate holdings to Divco West in a transaction valued around $1.3 billion. After the sale Berg held onto a few of his more prominent properties, including the Microsoft Campus in Mountain View, and is still actively involved with a number of his investment companies.

NED SPIEKER AND SPIEKER PROPERTIES

Ned Spieker in 1970 in front of a map highlighting his developments. Spieker Properties.

Ned Spieker was born in Orange County and moved to Atherton in 1948 where his dad made a living as a used car salesman. He relates that Atherton at the time was rural, similar to what Tracy is today. Spieker attended UC Berkley in the mid 1960s where he had his first foray into real estate. While president of a fraternity that was in dire straights financially and at risk of having to close their house, Spieker took to the streets seeking a summer tenant for their house to provide supplemental income. The tenant he finally secured was the newly formed Peace Corps.

A signed photograph from Trammell Crow which reads ' To Ned Spieker: My friend and the youngest partner we ever had'. Spieker Properties.

Spieker's creativity was rewarded a few years later when an alumni heard about it and offered him a job selling real estate. His first job was working for Dillingham and Associates where he helped develop Palo Alto Square on land they leased from Stanford University. He was then introduced to a Texas based developer by the name of Trammell Crow in 1970 and became his partner for Northern California for the next successful 16 years.

NED SPIEKER AND SPIEKER PROPERTIES

John French, Ned Spieker & Dennis Singleton shortly after forming Spieker Properties in the late 1980s. Spieker Properties.

In the midst of the savings and loan crisis of the late 1980s, Trammel Crow and Ned Spieker made an amicable split, divided their assets and Spieker took this opportunity to found Spieker Properties. In 1993 in the face of a tough lending market, Spieker took the company public as a means of raising additional operating capital. He recalls this period as the most risky and tense of his career. One of the characteristics that helped define Spieker's developments was his penchant for acquiring and controlling large amounts of product in a small geographic area, in essence creating a mini monopoly in any given sub-market.

A few of the buildings Spieker developed in the San Jose airport office market. Spieker Properties.

A great example of Spieker's real estate strategy can be found in the class A San Jose airport office market. This small market is comprised of under 20 buildings and is roughly three million square feet. During the heyday of Spieker Properties, he controlled 2.7 million square feet in that sub-market, roughly 90% of the inventory. By the time of the dot com bubble, Spieker had built his empire from 11 million square feet with a market capitalization of $800 million in 1993 to 42 million square feet with a market capitalization of $7.2 billion in 2001. At that point he decided to sell the company to Equity Office. The timing of the sale was very fortuitous as it closed only months before the dot.com bubble burst.

Network Room for the SAGE Computer System. IBM

In the early days of computers, due to their size and cost, only very large corporations and the U.S. Government could afford such machines. By far, the Defense Department was the computer's largest consumer. In the 1960s it is estimated that the Department of Defense owned more than 75% of all the computers in existence. A great example of a computer of the 1960s was the SAGE (Semi-Automatic Ground Environment), a multi-billion dollar state-of-the-art computerized air defense system acquired by the Air Force, in conjunction with MIT and IBM, at the beginning of The Cold War. Starting in 1958 the Air Force built around 20 SAGE centers across the U.S. Each center consisted of a four-story windowless building used to house all of the equipment related to the computer. The system cost the equivalent of $1.89 billion in today's dollars, occupied 113,000 square feet of floor space and contained 50,000 vacuum tubes.

Twelve: Mainframe Computers

IBM

"THINK" 1985!

IBM's General Products Division in San Jose. Voted "One of America's ten most beautiful plants" in the 1960s. IBM.

IBM's Building 25. Built in 1957 in the Edenvale district of San Jose, it was designed to be modernistic and was state of the art at the time. IBM.

An aerial view of IBM's South San Jose campus in 1974. IBM.

In 1952 IBM opened a West Coast laboratory in San Jose. The purpose of the new facility, deliberately removed from the mainstream IBM labs, was to seek and develop radically new information processing capabilities. When the operation grew from eight employees to 60 within the first year, IBM purchased 190 acres of land in the Edenvale area of South San Jose. Called building 25, the Cottle Road facility was designed to be modern and cutting edge. One of the most significant research projects in the early days was the invention of the hard disk drive. In 1960 an IBM 305 RAMAC was the first computer to tabulate scores at the Olympic Games. By the end of the 1960s IBM had close to 80% of the computer market and was one of the most successful and admired corporations in the world.

IBM

Introduced in 1956, the IBM 305 RAMAC (Random Access Memory Accounting System) was an electronic general purpose data processing machine that maintained business records on a real-time basis. The 305 RAMAC was one of the last vacuum tube systems designed by IBM, and more than 1,000 of them were built before production ended in 1961. IBM.

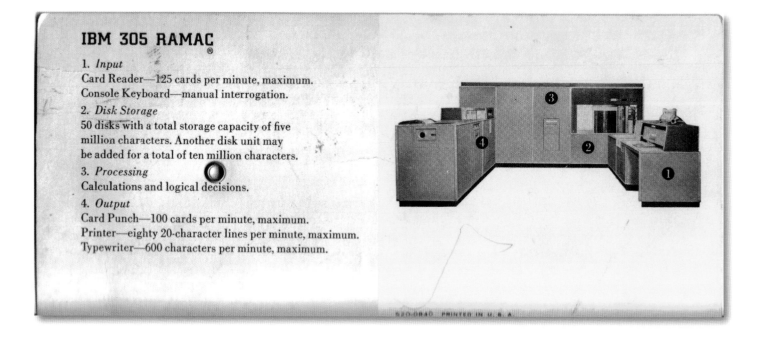

IBM 305 RAMAC ®

1. *Input*
Card Reader—125 cards per minute, maximum.
Console Keyboard—manual interrogation.

2. *Disk Storage*
50 disks with a total storage capacity of five million characters. Another disk unit may be added for a total of ten million characters.

3. *Processing*
Calculations and logical decisions.

4. *Output*
Card Punch—100 cards per minute, maximum.
Printer—eighty 20-character lines per minute, maximum.
Typewriter—600 characters per minute, maximum.

520-0840 PRINTED IN U. S. A.

In 1960 IBM's 305 RAMAC scored the Winter Olympic Games which were held in Lake Tahoe. The RAMAC also tallied votes for the presidential election that same year. IBM.

TANDEM COMPUTERS

Tandem Founders Mike Green, Jack Loustaunou, Jim Katzman, and Jimmy Treybig. Gaye Clemson.

In 1974 an article came out that claimed there would never be another computer company because IBM had eaten up the entire mainframe market. Incidentally, it was only months after this article was published that Tandem Computers was founded and soon became the dominant manufacturer of fault-tolerant computer systems for ATM networks, banks, and stock exchanges. Tandem Computers was founded by Jimmy Treybig, an eccentric Texan who first saw the market for ultra-reliable systems that would provide maximum uptime and zero data loss. Working in the commercial computing division at Hewlett Packard at the time, he mentioned this to his employer but they were not interested in developing that niche. Initial venture capital investment came from the investment firm, Kleiner Perkins. Treybig worked for Tom Perkins during Perkins' tenure at HP so Perkins had an appreciation for Treybig's business model: one that included detailed ideas for building a unique corporate culture for which Tandem became famous. One of the traditions that set Tandem apart was a weekly beer bust that included keg beer, wine, soft drinks, popcorn and unshelled peanuts. Besides being fun, the mixers encouraged employees of different groups and levels to learn what others in the company needed. Treybig was always present and accessible. Tandem was also a pioneer in granting stock options to all employees. In 1997 Tandem was acquired and it is now a server division within Hewlett Packard.

The first big system shipped to Ohio Community Libraries Cooperative. Gaye Clemson.

After an ad was published of two scantily clad women riding a tandem bicycle, the women in the marketing department were outraged and the result was the Incredible Hulk Contest where the male executives dressed scantily and were rated by the women of the company. Gaye Clemson.

TANDEM

ROLM

Rolm got its start in an old prune shack in Santa Clara. A symbol of the The Valley of Hearts Delight giving way to Silicon Valley. Pat Charles

ROLM was founded in 1969 and originally made customized and rugged computers for the US military and heavy commercial industries such as oil exploration. The company name was formed from the first letters of the founders names—Gene Richeson, Ken Oshman, Walter Loewenstern and Robert Maxfield—who were graduate students together at Stanford University. While not an original founder, Leo Chamberlain was hired on and became very much the soul of ROLM, advancing progressive workplace ideas such as GPW (Great Place to Work). Their campus on Old Ironsides Drive in Santa Clara was equipped with a swimming pool, open space park areas, a cafeteria and recreation center. In 1983 IBM partnered with, and later acquired, ROLM Corporation.

Rolm's Campus on Old Ironsides had lush landscaping, water features and plenty of outdoor seating and recreation areas. Pat Charles

Rolm's campus also featured a pool that the families of employees were encouraged to enjoy. Frequent water volleyball tournaments were hosted as a means of team bonding. Pat Charles

Rolm's lobby. Pat Charles

In 1975 Stanford engineering graduates developed the Altair, a $400 kit that included four circuit boards, and required the user to provide the monitor and keyboard. It became an instant hit with hobbyists, who bought thousands of kits in the first month. Intel.

The personal computer industry thrived because of the exponential growth in processing power of semiconductor chips, especially the single chip microprocessor introduced by Intel in 1971. Early personal computers were sold as kits and were used almost exclusively by hobbyists. In 1968 Hewlett Packard advertised their new 9100A programmable calculator as a "personal computer," but the term didn't resonate with their target audience, so they changed the name to the HP 9100A programmable calculator. By 1975 the term and the personal computer itself had developed a substantial audience. One of the first mainstream personal computers was the Altair 8800. This computer was developed by MIPS, a company founded by Stanford engineers that produced electronics kits for hobbyists. The Altair consisted of four circuit boards and cost $400. Because it was so affordable, it generated thousands of orders in the first month. By 1979 over half a million microcomputers were sold and the youth of the day experienced the power of the personal computer, an idea whose time had come. It was around this time that Steve Jobs and Steve Wozniak were attending Homebrew Computer Club meetings at Stanford University and developing the idea for the Apple I.

THIRTEEN: PERSONAL COMPUTING

Xerox PARC

In 1970 the Xerox Corporation assembled a world class team of experts in information and physical sciences to become "The Architects of Information," and established the company's Palo Alto Research Center with the mission statement, "To Create the Office of the Future." For their new research lab, Xerox leased 14 acres of land from Stanford University and agreed to build its facility deep into the site so as not to be visible from Page Mill Road. In 1971 Xerox PARC created the laser printer, which created a multi-billion dollar printing business for Xerox. Also in 1971, Xerox PARC designed Smalltalk, an object oriented programming language, which enabled computer programs to be improved without being entirely rewritten. This innovation revolutionized the software industry and influenced almost all subsequent programming systems. In 1974 Xerox PARC unveiled the Alto, the first workstation with a mouse, icons, pop-up menus, cut and paste, and overlapping windows, all of which could be controlled easily using a point and click technique. The engineers coined the phrase, "What You See Is What You Get," to describe the graphical elements on the screen and user-friendly experience. This graphical user interface influenced the development of all subsequent computer interfaces, including the famed Macintosh.

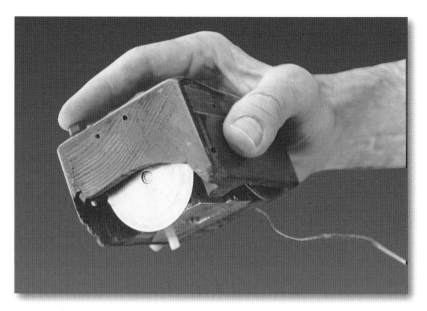

The first prototype of a mouse, created by Doug Engelbart with the Stanford Research Institute, which was licensed by both Xerox and Apple. SRI.

Xerox PARC's location in Stanford Research Park. Xerox PARC.

The Alto, created by Xerox PARC's engineers in 1974, was the first workstation with a mouse and point and click functionality. Xerox PARC.

ATARI

Atari founders Ted Dabney and Nolan Bushnell with Fred Marincic and Al Alcorn. While Dabney and Bushnell founded Atari in 1972, both would be gone from the company by 1980. Dabney left in 1973, believing the market was unstable; Bushnell left in 1979, after selling the company to Warner Communications.

THE NEWEST 2 PLAYER
VIDEO SKILL GAME

PONG

from ATARI CORPORATION
SYZYGY ENGINEERED

The Team That Pioneered Video Technology

FEATURES
- STRIKING Attract Mode
- Ball Serves Automatically
- Realistic Sounds of Ball Bouncing, Striking Paddle
- Simple to Operate Controls
- ALL SOLID STATE TV and Components for Long, Rugged Life
- ONE YEAR COMPUTER WARRANTY
- Proven HIGH PROFITS in Location After Location
- Low Key Cabinet, Suitable for Sophisticated Locations
- 25¢ per play

THIS GAME IS AVAILABLE FROM YOUR LOCAL DISTRIBUTOR

Manufactured by
ATARI, INC.
2962 SCOTT BLVD.
SANTA CLARA, CA.
95050

Maximum Dimensions:
WIDTH -26"
HEIGHT -50"
DEPTH -24
SHIPPING WEIGHT:
150 Lb.

In 1971 Nolan Bushnell and Ted Dabney designed and built the first arcade video game: Computer Space. In 1972 the pair founded Atari and soon hired Al Alcorn as their first design engineer. Bushnell decided to have Alcorn produce a game to test his abilities: from this training exercise came the arcade game Pong, an animated table tennis game. Atari placed the prototype in Andy Capp's Tavern in Sunnyvale to gage the public response. Legend has it that within the first week the bar owner called to complain that the machine was broken. When Alcorn investigated, he discovered the only problem was that the coin box was full. Pong was an overnight success and marked the start of the video game industry.

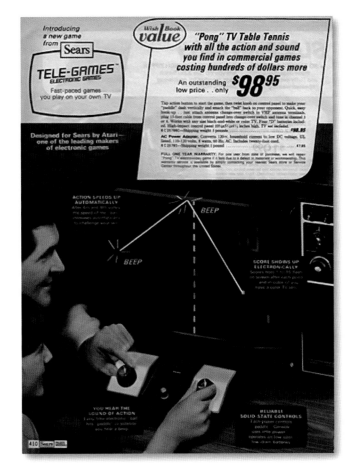

Pong advertisement in the Sears catalog.

Sears advertisement promoting a later version of the Atari video game console.

Nolan Bushnell was a larger than life character, and served as the company's spokesman. After the initial success of Pong, he went out in search of new capital to help propel the growth of his company. The problem he kept running into was that most investors saw the arcade game business as too capital intensive because large inventories were needed to support the business model. Then, Nolan met Don Valentine, who tells the story that when he went to check out Atari's assembly line in Los Gatos, he was nearly knocked over by the smell of marijuana. Undeterred, Valentine saw the real potential of the company to be in the recently developed, but not yet produced, home video console. He saw this console as having the ability to open up a new market segment and, assuming you could sell large quantities to retailers, could eliminate the need to house such large inventories. So, he provided the funding Atari needed. However, once the home console was produced, Bushnell found that retailers, including toy stores and electronics stores, didn't see the value in the product. This problem almost took the company down, until Valentine reached out to a friend who was a large investor in Sears. Thankfully, this call helped facilitate the exclusive distribution agreement between Atari and Sears, which was just in time for the 1975 Christmas season. To Bushnell and Valentine's delight, the home console was met with overwhelming demand from consumers.

APPLE

The Apple I was a fully assembled circuit board containing about 60+ chips. However, to make a working computer, users still had to add a case, power supply transformers, power switch, ASCII keyboard, and composite video display. Two hundred units sold in 1976.

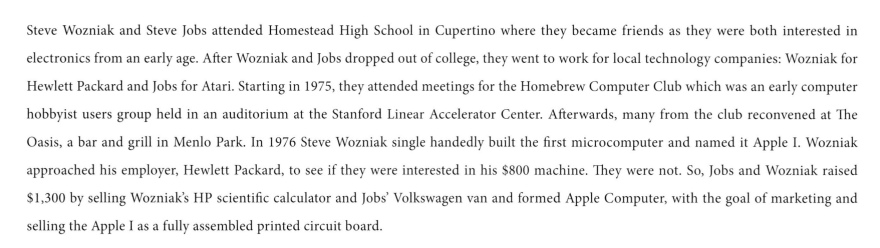

Steve Wozniak and Steve Jobs attended Homestead High School in Cupertino where they became friends as they were both interested in electronics from an early age. After Wozniak and Jobs dropped out of college, they went to work for local technology companies: Wozniak for Hewlett Packard and Jobs for Atari. Starting in 1975, they attended meetings for the Homebrew Computer Club which was an early computer hobbyist users group held in an auditorium at the Stanford Linear Accelerator Center. Afterwards, many from the club reconvened at The Oasis, a bar and grill in Menlo Park. In 1976 Steve Wozniak single handedly built the first microcomputer and named it Apple I. Wozniak approached his employer, Hewlett Packard, to see if they were interested in his $800 machine. They were not. So, Jobs and Wozniak raised $1,300 by selling Wozniak's HP scientific calculator and Jobs' Volkswagen van and formed Apple Computer, with the goal of marketing and selling the Apple I as a fully assembled printed circuit board.

Steve Jobs and Steve Wozniak.

Steve Jobs and Mike Markkula in 1977.

The market greeted the Apple I with open arms. With this initial success, Wozniak developed the Apple II in 1977. Once the Apple II had been developed, the partners arrived at a point where, in order to manufacture it, they needed funding. Steve Jobs approached Nolan Bushnell, his previous employer and founder of Atari, to see if he would like to make an investment in Apple. Bushnell was not interested but put Jobs in touch with Don Valentine of Sequoia Capital. Valentine, after meeting the young, unkempt Jobs asked, "Why did you send me this renegade from the human race?" Valentine was also not interested in funding Apple, but put Jobs in touch with Mike Markkula who had made millions on stock options from positions he held at Fairchild Semiconductor and Intel. Markkula was convinced of the market for the Apple II, and personal computers in general. Markkula committed $142,000 to the venture, became a one-third owner of Apple and employee number three. Markkula served as Chairman of the Board from 1985 until 1997. In 1979 Steve Jobs visited Xerox PARC and after getting a tour of the Xerox Alto, he went on to redefine personal computing modeled on the graphic user interface of the Alto. By 1980 Apple was up to several thousand employees and went public for a record $1.3 billion.

TIMELINE OF APPLE PRODUCTS

The Macintosh became the first commercially successful personal computer to feature a mouse and a graphical user interface, a feature Jobs initially saw at Xerox PARC years before. Initial price tag: $3,195.

Ahead of its time, Apple introduced the Newton and coined the term PDA—Personal Digital Assistant. While the Newton did not become a success, the term PDA stuck. Initial price tag: $699.

1984

1993

1991

1998

When first introduced, the Powerbook line was revolutionary with its built-in trackball and innovative palm rest area with the keyboard behind. All future notebooks would follow this new design. Initial price tag: $2,500.

The iMac was unveiled after Jobs returned to Apple. It was considered one of their most innovative computers since the original Macintosh in 1984. It was aimed at the low-end consumer market and was designed with navigating the Internet in mind. Initial price tag: $1,299.

The introduction of the first iPod with a remarkable 5 gigabytes of storage revolutionized the music market. Initial price tag: $399.

The MacBook Air was introduced as the worlds lightest computer that still maintained performance. Initial price tag: $1799.

2001

2008

2007

2010

After much anticipation, the iPhone introduction took the market by storm. Initial price tag: $399.

The most anticipated device since Steve Jobs killed the Newton, his first act as CEO when he rejoined the company. Initial price tag for the iPad: $499.

STEVE JOBS

Steve Jobs' senior portrait from Homestead High School, class of 1972. Even as a child, Steve Jobs was interested in electronics. In fact, he was only 13 when he called Bill Hewlett at home and asked if he could have some spare parts for a frequency counter.

Steve Jobs and "frenemy," Bill Gates in 1985. The complex relationship between the two men began in the late 1970s when Microsoft was writing most of the software for the Apple II. Over the years, their relationship fluctuated between partners and rivals, which included both a mutual respect and cut throat competition. Supposedly, the last meeting between the two took place at Jobs' home a few months before he died.

Steve Jobs in 1980. He credits part of his success to using various seemingly unrelated experiences, to influence his products. An example he often cited was the calligraphy class he took in college, which later inspired the beautiful typography incorporated into the Macintosh.

Think different.

After being ousted from Apple by John Sculley in 1985, Jobs founded NeXT Computer. Ten years later, Apple Computer announced an intention to acquire NeXT for the purpose of using the NeXT software platform to replace the dated Mac OS. After the acquisition, Jobs returned to Apple as a consultant and shortly thereafter became the de facto CEO.

In 1986 Jobs acquired the computer graphics division of Lucasfilm, which was spun off as Pixar. He was credited in Toy Story (1995) as an executive producer. He served as CEO and majority shareholder until Disney's purchase of Pixar in 2006.

▶

Jobs died at his Palo Alto home on October 5, 2011, due to complications with pancreatic cancer. Both Apple and Microsoft flew their flags at half-staff throughout their respective headquarters and campuses. The Governor of California, Jerry Brown, declared Sunday, October 16, 2011 "Steve Jobs Day." A private memorial service for Apple employees was held on October 19, 2011, on the Apple Campus in Cupertino as seen here.

ADOBE SYSTEMS

Adobe's first office in Mountain View on Marine Way, circa 1982.
Adobe Systems.

Adobe founders, John Warnock and Charles Geshke. Adobe Systems.

In 1982 John Warnock and Charles Geschke left Xerox PARC to found Adobe Systems. The company name comes from the Adobe Creek in Los Altos, which ran behind both founders' homes. Their first product was the PostScript page description language, which described to a printer the appearance of a printed page. Adobe's Postscript language went on the market in 1984. Around the same time, Steve Jobs approached Adobe and urged them to adapt PostScript to be used as the language driving laser printers. In March 1985 the Apple LaserWriter was the first printer to ship with PostScript, sparking the desktop publishing revolution in the mid-1980s. The next move for Adobe was a to enter the consumer software market with Adobe Illustrator, a vector-based drawing program for the Apple Macintosh. In 1989 Adobe introduced what was to become its flagship product, an image-editing program for the Macintosh called Photoshop. In 1993 Adobe introduced PDF, the Portable Document Format: and Adobe Acrobat/Reader software, which became an international standard. As of 2010 Adobe Systems had over 9,000 employees, about 40% of whom work in San Jose.

Adobe PostScript

PostScript Language

1984

Adobe Photoshop

1989

Adobe PageMaker

1994

1986

Adobe Illustrator

1993

Adobe PDF

1999

Adobe InDesign

Adobe now occupies three high rise buildings in downtown San Jose totaling around 1 million square feet. The buildings are known for their green design and in 2006 the towers were awarded The Leadership in Energy and Environmental Design (LEED) Platinum Certification by the United States Green Building Council. Adobe Systems.

SUN MICROSYSTEMS

Founders of Sun Microsystems in 1982. From left: Vinod Khosla, Bill Joy, Andy Bechtolsheim and Scott McNealy.

Sun Microsystems was founded by Stanford graduate students, Vinod Khosla, Andy Bechtolsheim, and Scott McNealy in 1982. The initial design for what became Sun's first Unix workstation, the Sun-1, was conceived by Andy Bechtolsheim while he was still at Stanford, and is aptly named SUN for "'Stanford University Network." Like Steve Jobs before him, Bechtolsheim had access to the research facilities at Xerox PARC and the design of the Sun-1 was based loosely around the Xerox Alto. Shortly after the inception of Sun Microsystems, Bill Joy, a graduate student from Berkeley, joined the company and is considered one of the original founders. Sun Microsystems is also well known for the Java platform they developed in the early 1990s. Java is an object-oriented programming language which continues to be one of the world's most popular programming languages. Unfortunately, starting in the mid 1990s, Sun Microsystems expanded too rapidly and once the dot.com bubble burst, they found themselves over extended on real estate obligations and sitting inventory. Sun was never quite able to fully recover and was acquired by Oracle in 2010. The four original founders have all moved on to new high profile ventures: Andy Bechtolsheim founded Arista Networks; Vinod Khosla founded the venture capital firm Khosla Ventures; Scott McNealy served as Sun's CEO for 22 years, a record in Silicon Valley, and has recently founded a social media company; and Bill Joy is now a partner at Kleiner Perkins Caufield Byers.

Agnews Insane Asylum in 1896 prior to its destruction in 1906.

The Agnews clock tower, completed in 1911.

Sun's headquarters. Built in 1997 and now occupied by Oracle following their acquisition of Sun.

The campus that Sun Microsystems developed in Santa Clara has a long history. Initially, the land was occupied by Agnews Insane Asylum. Developed in 1885, it was an imposing red brick building which was known at the time as "The Great Asylum for the Insane." After the 1906 earthquake, the center became infamous as it was the site of Santa Clara Valley's greatest loss of life resulting from the quake: 117 patients and staff were killed, and buried in mass graves on the site. The main building was irreparably damaged and had to be rebuilt. In 1911 the center reopened and was renamed Agnews State Mental Hospital. It was constructed in the Spanish Colonial Revival style in a layout resembling a college campus. At the time, it boasted the largest population in the South San Francisco Bay Area and was a small self-contained town with shops, a farm, a power plant, a fire department and its own train station. In 1926 Agnews expanded to include a second campus in San Jose to treat those with developmental disabilities. The original Agnews campus in Santa Clara closed in 1997. At that time, the State of California sold 82 acres to Sun Microsystems for their headquarters, with the condition that Sun would restore four of the historic buildings for public use.

"The van where the Internet was born". SRI.

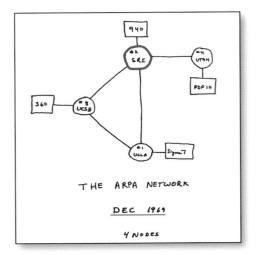

The hand sketched design of the ARPANET, which transmitted the first message over an electronic computer network in 1977. SRI.

In 1958 the Russians launched Sputnik, the first earth orbiting satellite. In response, the U.S. Government created a new task force, the Defense Advanced Research Projects Agency or DARPA, whose mission was to expand the frontiers of technology and science as a matter of national defense. One of DARPA's projects was the ARPANET which was the precursor to the Internet we know today. The first true Internet transmission occurred in November 1977 when SRI originated the first connection between three disparate networks. However, it wasn't until the mid 1990s that the concept of the Internet really took shape and began its rapid expansion. During the early years of the Internet, most people connected over a phone line with a dial-up 56K modem. To put this into context, that is almost two thousand times slower than connections today. In 1995 about 10% of adults in the U.S. were going online. By 2011 that figure had jumped to 78% of adults and 95% of teenagers.

FOURTEEN: THE INTERNET

STANFORD RESEARCH INSTITUTE

Doug Engelbart at SRI, showcasing the first computer mouse which he designed. SRI.

In 1946 the trustees of Stanford University established Stanford Research Institute in Menlo Park as a nonprofit organization to serve as a center of innovation to support economic development in the region. To this day, SRI International, as it is now known, remains one of the largest contract research institutes in the world. It performs client-sponsored research and development for government agencies, commercial businesses, and private foundations. It also licenses its technologies, forms strategic partnerships, and creates spin-off companies. One of the most famous alumni is Doug Engelbart, the main innovator of modern computer-human interface elements including: bit-mapped displays, collaboration software, hypertext, and the computer mouse. He was awarded the National Medal of Technology and Innovation in 2000 and passed away in 2013.

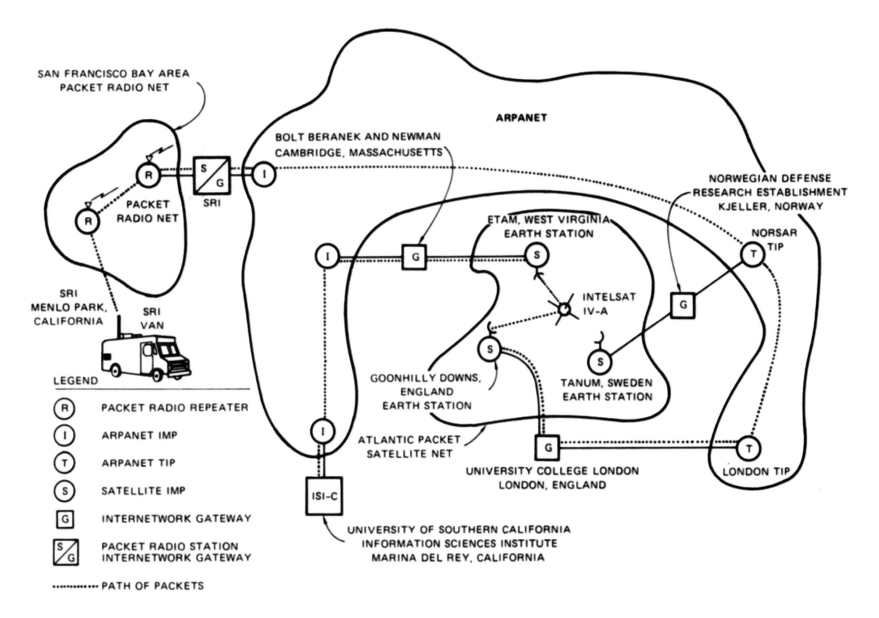

A schematic of the 1977 connection between three disparate networks. SRI.

Stanford Research Institute also had its hands in the beginning of the Internet. In October 1969 the world's first electronic computer network, ARPANET, was established between nodes at UCLA and Douglas Engelbart's lab at SRI. The first message on the ARPANET was sent by a UCLA student with the message text 'login'. The l and the o letters were transmitted, but the system then crashed. Hence, the literal first message sent over the ARPANET was lo. The first true Internet transmission occurred in November 1977, when SRI originated the first connection between three disparate networks. Data flowed seamlessly through a mobile van between SRI in Menlo Park, California and the University of Southern California in Los Angeles via London, England, across three types of networks: packet radio, satellite, and the ARPANET.

NETSCAPE

Netscape's Jim Clark, left, and Marc Andreessen pose outside of their offices in Mountain View.

Born in 1971, Marc Andreessen was raised in the Midwest and attended the University of Illinois receiving a bachelor's degree in computer science. While an undergraduate, he worked at the National Center for Supercomputing Applications (NCSA) which was located on campus. There he became familiar with standards for the World Wide Web. He and co-worker Eric Bina worked on creating a user-friendly web browser containing a graphical user interface. The resulting code was the Mosaic Web Browser. After Andreessen graduated in 1993, he moved to California and met with Jim Clark, the recently departed founder of Silicon Graphics. Clark believed that the Mosaic browser had great commercial possibilities and suggested starting an Internet software company. Clark helped secure funding from Kleiner Perkins Caufield & Byers and soon Mosaic Communications Corporation was in business.

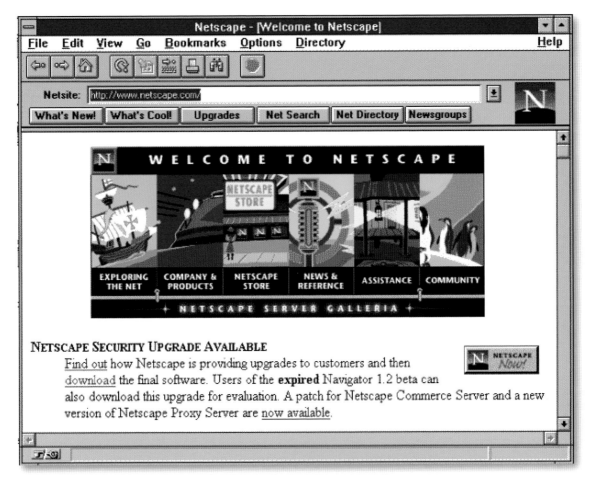

The original Netscape Internet browser.

The company soon changed its name to Netscape Communications, and its flagship Web browser was the Netscape Navigator. Netscape made a very successful IPO in 1995. The stock was initially priced at $14 per share and closed at $58.25 that same day, creating a market value of $2.9 billion. The runaway success of Netscape's IPO turned Andreessen into the poster-boy wunderkind of the Internet generation: twenty-something, high-tech, ambitious, and worth millions (or billions) of dollars practically overnight. Netscape's success attracted the attention of Microsoft, which recognized the Web's potential and wanted to put itself at the forefront of the rising Internet revolution. Microsoft licensed the Mosaic source code from the University of Illinois, and turned it into Internet Explorer. The resulting battle between the two companies became known as the Browser Wars. Netscape was acquired in 1999 for $4.2 billion by AOL, which made Andreessen its Chief Technology Officer. Marc Andreessen went on to found the venture capital firm Andreessen Horowitz in 2009 with partner Ben Horowitz, and the pair have since invested in companies such as Twitter, Groupon, Skype and Zynga.

YAHOO!

David Filo and Jerry Yang in 1997 with a fish prop in Yahoo!'s early office located at 3400 Central Expressway in Santa Clara.

David Filo and Jerry Yang in front of their Yahoo logo.

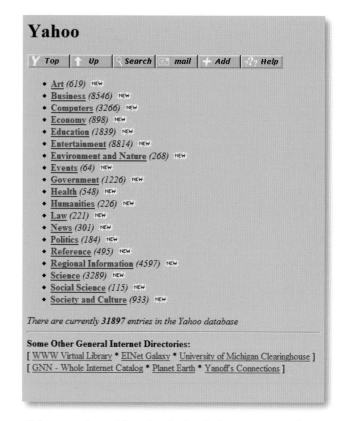

Yahoo started as a side project for Stanford engineering students, called "David and Jerry's Guide to the World Wide Web," as a way for them to organize the websites they frequented.

The Yahoo campus located off Highway 101 and Mathilda Avenue in Sunnyvale. The company currently occupies 800,000 square feet, which was developed for them in 2000.

Jerry Yang and David Filo were electrical engineering graduate students at Stanford University. In 1994, while trying to organize their personal interests on the Internet, they created a website they called, "David and Jerry's Guide to the World Wide Web." It was a directory of other websites, organized in a hierarchy with categories and subcategories. They soon found that they had a loyal following of people who also wanted a single place to find useful Web sites. Later that year, they renamed their site to "Yahoo!" which is an acronym for "Yet Another Hierarchical Officious Oracle." The founders say they also liked the name based on the definition of a yahoo: "rude, unsophisticated, uncouth." Yahoo!'s fan base continued to grow and within six months their site was receiving 1,000,000 hits per day. With such an enthusiastic reception, the pair incorporated the business and raised a $2 million round of funding from Sequoia Capital in 1995. The site's popularity grew exponentially, and with only 49 employees they went public in 1996. The company was hit hard by the dot.com bust and has gone through a number of management changes during the last decade. Most recently they appointed former Google executive Marissa Mayer, to the post of CEO. Yahoo! is headquartered in Sunnyvale and employs over 10,000 people worldwide.

eBAY

eBay founder Pierre Omidyar and former CEO Meg Whitman. eBay.

eBay was founded in 1995 by Pierre Omidyar under the name, AuctionWeb. Pierre started the site as an experiment: what would happen if everyone in the world had equal access to a single global marketplace? Pierre tested his new auction website by posting a broken laser pointer for sale. To his surprise, a collector bought it for $14.83. And so began a radical transformation in commerce. In less than a year and with only a few employees, eBay was seeing $10,000 per month in revenue and had 41,000 registered users. eBay's growth continued exponentially from there, and by 1997 they were hosting 200,000 auctions per month: ten times the volume of just a year before. In 1998 Meg Whitman joined eBay as CEO and later that year, eBay went public. By 1999 there were 10 million registered users, $2.8 billion in Gross Merchandise Volume and 640 employees. In 2002 eBay acquired the online payment company, PayPal, which secured eBay's position as the number one eCommerce site. By 2005 eBay employed over 10,000 people worldwide.

eBay's campus in Campbell has named their buildings after the categories of the items they sell.

In 1997 eBay celebrated the sale of it's one millionth item: A Big Bird toy. eBay.

The highest priced item sold to date: in 2001 a Gulfstream jet for $4.9 million.

In 2008 an eBay auction for lunch with Warren Buffett raised $2.1 million for charity.

GOOGLE

Where it all started: Susan Wojcicki's garage in Menlo Park. Google.

In 1999, with only 8 employees, Google left the garage for their first corporate location: 165 University Avenue in Palo Alto. Google.

In 1995 while studying for a graduate degree in computer science at Stanford University, Larry Page and Sergey Brin began collaborating on a search engine they called BackRub and operated it on Stanford servers. A year after the launch of the search engine, it was already taking up too much bandwidth for the University. So, in 1997 the two engineers decided to take their search engine out of Stanford and commercialize it. They named the company Google — a play on the word googol, which is a mathematical term for the number one followed by one hundred zeros. The use of the term reflects their mission to organize a seemingly infinite amount of information on the web. In 1998 Sun co-founder Andy Bechtolsheim gave Sergey and Larry $100,000 to get the company off the ground. The company first started in Susan Wojcicki's garage (sister of Sergey Brin's wife, Anne Wojcicki) in Menlo Park. Only a few months after incorporating, PC Magazine named Google the search engine of choice. In 1999 with only eight employees, Google left the garage for their first corporate location: 165 University Avenue in Palo Alto. Within a few months, the company announced a $25 million round of funding from Sequoia Capital and Kleiner Perkins, as well as the need to relocate the corporate location again due to their expanding workforce. With over 35 employees, Google moved to the Shoreline district of Mountain View, with their first building located at 2400 E. Bayshore Road. With this move they hired their first corporate chef, Charlie Ayers, whose initial claim to fame was catering for the Grateful Dead. By the year 2000 Google had returned over a billion search results and became the world's largest search engine.

From left to right: Eric Schmidt, Larry Page and Sergey Brin in their experimental self-driving car.

Communal bikes provided by Google for employees to travel around the campus.

Google's iconic Shoreline campus in Mountain View.

Aerial view of the Mountain View campus where most buildings are powered with solar panels.

LinkedIn

LinkedIn was founded in 2002 by Reid Hoffman. Hoffman was born in Palo Alto and grew up in Berkeley. He attended Stanford University and in 1994 joined Apple Computer where he worked on eWorld, an early attempt at creating a social network. In 1997 Hoffman continued his quest to improve online networking and co-founded his first company, Socialnet.com, an online dating service where people were matched up based on similar interests. While still at Socialnet.com, Hoffman joined the board of directors at the newly founded

PayPal and shortly thereafter left Socialnet.com to join PayPal full-time as the company's COO in 2000. After Paypal was acquired by eBay in 2002, he founded LinkedIn along with a team he assembled from PayPal and Socialnet.com. The principal investment came from Sequoia Capital. Reid served as CEO for the first four years and is currently Chairman of the Board. The site officially launched in May 2003, and within a month the site had a total of 4,500 members in the network. LinkedIn reached profitability in March of 2006 and went public in 2011. LinkedIn has recently built a new 500,000 square foot campus in Sunnyvale and as of as of 2013 reported more than 225 million users.

The LinkedIn team posing in front of their Mountain View campus at the 5 million user milestone. LinkedIn.

The LinkedIn team posing in front of their Mountain View campus at the 150 million user milestone. LinkedIn.

FACEBOOK

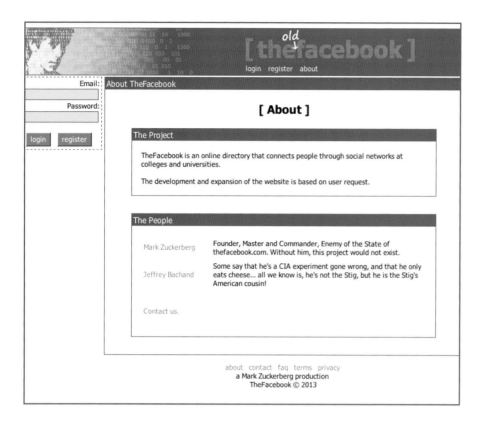

The original login page for "thefacebook," while still operating out of Harvard. Facebook.

Mark Zuckerberg in his Palo Alto Offices before the company relocated to Menlo Park. Facebook.

In 2003 Harvard Student, Mark Zuckerberg, came up with Facemash, an online game for Harvard students that allowed participants to compare two student pictures side-by-side and choose who was "hot" and who was "not." The website gained overnight popularity within the student body but was soon shut down by Harvard executives. Zuckerberg faced charges of violating copyrights, breach of security, and violating individual privacy, for which he faced expulsion from the University. Charges were eventually dropped. In February of 2004 Zuckerberg launched "thefacebook," which was an early version of what Facebook is today and only available to Harvard students. With the launch of the site: three of Zuckerberg's classmates joined his team, Andrew McCollum, Chris Hughes and Dustin Moskovitz. With the launch of the site, three Harvard students (Cameron & Tyler Winklevoss and Divya Narendra) accused Zuckerberg of intentionally misleading them into believing that he would help them build a social network called HarvardConnection.com. They claimed that instead, he used their idea to build a competing product. Nonetheless, within the first month of the launch of thefacebook, more than half the undergraduate population at Harvard was registered on the service. Later in 2004 Facebook expanded its reach into all Ivy League and Boston-area schools and gradually reached most universities in the United States and Canada.

The original Facebook offices on University Avenue in downtown Palo Alto. Facebook.

Current Facebook headquarters in the old Sun Campus in East Menlo Park. Facebook.

In the summer of 2004 Facebook was incorporated and relocated its headquarters to Palo Alto. Around this time Sean Parker, the man behind Napster, joined the team as the company's first president, in charge of helping to raise the necessary capital. Sean Parker initially approached Reid Hoffman, the CEO of LinkedIn. While Hoffman liked Facebook, he declined to be the lead investor due to a potential conflict of interest. Instead, Hoffman redirected Parker to Peter Thiel, whom Reid knew from his days at PayPal, and Thiel provided the first angel investment of $500,000. In 2005 the company dropped "the" from its name and raised an additional $12.7 million from Accel Partners, which at the time gave Facebook a $98 million valuation. In 2006 Facebook expanded out of the strictly college market and granted access to everyone over the age of 13. It was around this time that they raised an additional $27.5 million, placing the company at a $500 million valuation. In May 2012 Facebook went public raising $16 billion, the third largest in U.S. history. Despite this achievement, their public offering was plagued with issues: including technical problems and lack of public support for the initial offering price. However, the company was able to recover and as of June 2014, has a market capitalization of over $160 billion.

Index

BIBLIOGRAPHY

<u>BOOKS:</u>

The Silicon Valley Edge; A Habitat for Innovation and Entrepreneurship

Edited by Chong-Moon Lee, William F. Miller, Marguerite Gong Hancock and Henry S. Rowen

Stanford University Press, 2000

Understanding Silicon Valley; The Anatomy of an Entrepreneurial Region

Edited by Martin Kenney

Stanford University Press, 2000

Reconstructing Early Historical Landscapes in the Northern Santa Clara Valley

Author Alan K. Brown

Santa Clara University, Department of Anthropology and Sociology, 2005

Old Santa Clara Valley : a guide to historic buildings from Palo Alto to Gilroy

Author Phyllis Filiberti Butler

Wide World Publisher/Tetra, 1991

Technology, Entrepreneurs and Silicon Valley

Authors John McLaughlin and Carol Whiteley

Santa Clara Valley Historical Society, 2002

Silicon Valley : 110 Year Renaissance

John McLaughlin, Leigh Weimers, Ward Winslow

Santa Clara Valley Historical Society, 2008

A History of Silicon Valley

Piero Scaruffi (Author), Arun Rao (Author)

Omniware Group, 2011

Sunshine, Fruit and Flowers: Santa Clara County and Its Resources; Historical, Descriptive, Statistical

A Souvenir of the San Jose Mercury, 1895 (Hardcover)

WEBSITES:

www.siliconvalleyhistorical.org/

www.npr.org/starting-up-silicon-valleys-origins

www.steveblank.com/category/secret-history-of-silicon-valley/

www.wikipedia.org

FILMS:

Pirates of Silicon Valley (TV 1999)

PBS' American Experience: Silicon Valley

Something Ventured (2011)